SHOOTING TYPES:
THE SECOND BARREL

ACKNOWLEDGEMENTS

Grateful thanks are due to *The Shooting Gazette* and its Editor, Will Hetherington, for supporting the publication of this second collection of *Shooting Types* and, critically, for encouraging us to continue sending up his readership in the magazine.

The most appreciation, however, must go to all those kind hosts and hostesses, fellow Guns, diligent keepers, hardworking beaters and pickers-up – and their dogs - who provide us with days of fun and yards of material.

Thank you all.

Giles Catchpole and Bryn Parry

SHOOTING TYPES:
THE SECOND BARREL

GILES CATCHPOLE
& BRYN PARRY

Quiller

Text copyright © 2011 Giles Catchpole
Illustrations copyright © 2011 Bryn Parry

First published in the UK in 2011
by Quiller, an imprint of Quiller Publishing Ltd

British Library Cataloguing-in-Publication Data
  A catalogue record for this book
  is available from the British Library

ISBN 978 1 84689 113 7

Printed in China

Quiller

An imprint of Quiller Publishing Ltd
Wykey House, Wykey, Shrewsbury, SY4 1JA
Tel: 01939 261616 Fax: 01939 261606
E-mail: info@quillerbooks.com
Website: www.countrybooksdirect.com

CONTENTS

HARD MEN

Vince and Terry are hard men. You've probably seen them on the beating line. Raggedy leggings and a worn Barbour over a shirt that is more open than not. But good boots. Hard men have an appreciation for the quality of the necessities. Proper job, son. They are largely impervious to cold. There is probably a spaniel somewhere in the vicinity.

The boys divide their time between working off-shore and the haulage business. So it's month on, month off on the rigs and the rest of the time freelancing on the HGVs. Which means that they are not short of the readies betimes – hence the good boots. And the L200 Warrior pick-up, or as it might be the mighty Nissan Navarra, in which they roll into the farmyard. But at weekends in the winter they beat, and their girls pick up. That's Jacqui back there behind you with the Labs and Fran's working over on the next estate today. They shoot three days a week there, which keeps her busy.

And if you should happen to be the walking Gun, you might find out how hard they are.

'I wen' over to feed Father's old boar afore I come out today. Blas' he en't half an ugly old sod. An' he wus lookin' uglier than ever t'day. Come at me soon as I got me leg ower the fence.' 'Did he have you then, Vinny boy?' 'Naw. Give the old bugger one in the snout wi' the bucket t' giv' 'im the turnabout an' another in the tackle wi' me boot t' teach 'im a lesson. Proper job.'

'Ere, Tel, you bin barred from the Horse-shoes, 'ave you?'

'Well, me an' Vinny goes in there and some bugger says we 'ad to beat 'im afore we get on the pool table. So Vin gives 'im a pop wi' 'is cue an' I says to 'im, "That's yew beat, matey!" an' 'e goes bleating to the brewery. So we's out for three months.'

And that's the point about hard men. They don't waste time in idle chatter. You poke these boys in the chest and they'll twat you right back. They don't argue, they act. They don't threaten, they deliver. Just like that. No worries. Proper job.

But these are the guys you need for the poacher patrols when the poult snatchers venture into the vicinity. Or when the longdog men come down after the hares. The community wildlife officer may be all very well for nine to five but after dark in the larches it's the hard men you want to get stuff sorted out in short order. No nonsense.

They were a tasty pair when they were younger, as some recall. They did get into some mischief, that's for sure. But these days they are strictly on the up. With the money they make, they scarcely need to do otherwise. Though they are not above doing a deal here and there, if you know what they mean. But they don't pull any strokes, no more. And they don't start stuff no more. Though they are more than capable of finishing it. And they are a highlight of the

county fair. Arm wrestling
all comers for a pound
a go for the Game
Conservancy and
they're a fixture in
the final of the
bale tossing.
Though it is said
they take it in turns to
win.

And, of course, they
are always there or
thereabouts at the
local clay shoots in the
summer. Beretta vests,
John Deere caps, Berm-
udas. With nice guns.
And good boots, of course.
Hard men know the value of
good gear. Proper job.

THE BOYS' SHOOT

Where did this idea of the boys' shoot come from anyway? I'm all for encouraging the young and passing on the many and manifest benefits of our country sports. I think that taking a few youngsters for a bit of an armed maraud about the hedges and ditches between Christmas and New Year is a good way of dragging them away from the latest Grand Theft Auto shoot 'em up 'puter game and forcing some fresh air and social responsibility into them while working a bit of the Christmas pud off one's own waistline. But this is a full-fledged driven day. I was in my twenties before ever I got to go on a driven shoot; and I had to pay for it myself. And here are a bunch of teenagers staring down the barrel of five drives with elevenses and lunch and a bag that runs into three figures. It's not fair. And if that sounds like whining... well, I don't care. So there.

It's good fun for all that and I don't really begrudge them it. Much.

What strikes me most forcibly, though, is how middle-aged they are already. I know that children, youngsters, kids – call them what you like – grow up faster than ever the rest of us did but as they lounge against the shoot wagon in their tweeds and flat caps, slugging shandies and munching sausages, this lot are in their mid-teens at best and they already sound fifty.

'So how's tricks with you these days, Justin?'

'Well, grinding on, old boy. Grinding on. Managed to knock off the GCSEs in the summer, y'know.'

'As and Bs, I s'pose?'

'Yeah. Dropped one on the science side but straighted the rest, so no worries really. But the workload for A-levels is really, like, severe.'

'Tell me about it. It took me, like, hours just to download my coursework. Doing much shooting then?'

'Well, I had a day with Jacko before Christmas and I'm going to Cazzers next week. You there?'

'Can't, mate. We'll be in Chamonix. Dad says that there is no point having a chalet if we don't use it.'

'True. True. We're going to Verbier at Easter with Bella and Charlie.'

'Their dad is your uncle, right?'

'Godfather. I had to, like, do work experience with him this summer. He's got this really cool office in the City.'

'What's he do, then?'

'No idea, mate, but he's got this, like, huge media centre in his room with, like, 40 inch multi-screens and everything. An' it's all wireless and bluetoothed and everything. State of the art, man, state of the art. And he, like, just stares at it all day and then makes a couple of calls and goes out to lunch. And he's loaded, right? That's what I wanna do, man. Whatever it is.'

'Too right, mate. I spent a couple of weeks with Jason's old man, y'know. He's a lawyer. He charges his customers hundreds of pounds an hour and all he does is copy the answers out of old books. And he has a yacht.'

A tweedy retainer emerges from the undergrowth and encourages them to embus for the next drive.

'Hey ho! Back into the firing line, chaps. Make sure you have plenty of shells this could be the big first half closer. Dad says they took fifty or more off this drive when he was here. I wonder what's for lunch?'

Whatever will they be like when they really are fifty, I wonder? Much like us, I suppose. Scary.

GUN ERRANT

He is the wandering Gun. During the shooting season Christopher is a nomad. Or perhaps he is nearer to a pilgrim, since his grail is the next shoot and he criss-crosses the land in pursuit of it. Sometimes he joins a group of chums on a let day but more often he is an invited guest. Here and there. Everywhere, actually. The reason that he is invited is because he has bags of charm. And he shoots awfully well, of course. Awfully well. Beautifully, in fact. He's just a joy to watch. And he has a brilliant dog too who is his constant companion on the long journeys from the west country to the West Ridings by way of the Cotswolds and the Welsh borders and then on to Scotland and beyond to the isles and the wildfowling there before turning south once more to call in at Northumberland, Yorkshire, Lincolnshire and into East Anglia. And round and round and up and down. All over the place. Moving on. The wandering Gun.

No one knows very much about him. Christopher, Chris, Christophe, Christian; his fellow Guns know him by different soubriquets – though the dog is known to all as Sergeant. 'In you go, Sergeant. Fetch him out. There's a good fellow.'

Which makes many of the chaps think that Christopher might have been in the army. Jeremy insists that Chris was a Blue and Royal, although Russell insists that Michael assured him that he was a Lifeguard. An assertion that Jonno's wife Debbie dismisses out of hand because her best friend Laura insists she was bowled over by him in full regimental fig at a highland regiment's ball when she was trailing an affair with a Scots Guard.

Whereas Jimmy, who knows everyone and everything, insists that they were at Oxford together.

What everyone knows is that they have met Christopher shooting something somewhere.

Equally there is some doubt about what Chris actually does. Outside of the shooting season that is. He mentions the law but never offers specifics. So whether he makes it, applies it or maybe even breaks it is never clear. Whatever it is, it leaves him plenty of time to shoot. And it must pay reasonably well because Chris is always armed with magnums of the good stuff. The cartridge bill must be going a bit too. And the guns are high end, though old. And yet, and at the same time, his car is an aging Mercedes estate and his suit, though well cut, is not in its first flush. Though whose is? Doesn't really answer the question, does it?

Then there are the girls. Young, not so young, of mature years. Invariably introduced as just friends. Always pretty, always charming and all clearly devoted to Christopher. Is he really just giving her a lift to Cheshire just because they have both been invited coincidentally to the same house for the weekend and the shooting? The boys are agog with jealousy and the wives

are just fascinated. And yet no one ever seems to get to the bottom of it. As it were.

Not least because there is little time. He's here, he's there, he shoots, he lunches, he charms, he tips – and then he moves on. He is the wandering Gun.

WILD MEN

We know that gamekeepers come in all shapes and sizes but we also know that they are all dedicated to the preservation of game. Hence the name. Gamekeepers. Some, though, preserve game by rearing birds. Some from the egg and some from poults brought in from the game farmer. And preserved. And fed and watered. And watched and nursed. And preserved. And that is the keeper's way. And his life. Feeding and watering. Watching and preserving. Rearing and keeping.

But there is another breed of keeper whose life is different. There are shoots out there where the birds are wild. As it might be on the moors, of course, where the wild grouse call. But also in the lowlands; deep in the borders perhaps or out in the Fens, on the rich, dark lands of East Anglia; in the Black Mountains of Wales. Here and there. On the outskirts. In the wilder parts of the country.

And in these places the keepers do not rear. Here the birds, be they grouse, be they pheasants or be they partridge, rear themselves in the natural old fashioned way. Nesting and brooding. Feeding and watering themselves and their little ones.

And these keepers devote their energies to the unremitting war on vermin. Rats, grey squirrels, magpies, crows, gulls and jays. The weasel, the stoat, the blasted mink. The foxes and cats. These are the wild men; and they are different. They live by the trap and the gun. And the war goes on all day every day. He puts down rat baits by the ton on the mile after mile of hedgerows that are his domain. His trap lines run into hundreds, every one checked morning and evening and emptied, re-baited and reset. The baiting alone requires regular forays after the rabbits. Fifty here, a hundred there. Puttering around the estate on the quad bike in the gloaming with a silenced .410 to collect the necessary. And not just for the traps, of course, but to maintain the buffer feeding for the buzzards and the owls and the kites and the harriers which must be bribed with regular offerings to leave the game be, since they cannot be otherwise controlled despite exploding numbers.

Dawn finds him on the pig units with a sack of shells and his trusty auto. The wild men have no fancy guns. For them the shotgun is a tool and only a tool and the need to shoot fast and recoil free outweighs any aesthetic consideration. Fast and straight is all that he requires when he is taking out two hundred voracious predators at a session. Then it is round the trap lines again before applying himself to the habitat improvement that takes up the rest of his time. As it might be planting new grasses here for the benefit of the little partridges of felling a bit of a clearing there to encourage new ground growth for nest sites for the pheasants; and to encourage the butterflies, of course. Not that he cares much for the butterflies – though they are nice to see about the place – but their larvae are perfect chick food, after all, so the more the merrier.

And then there are the foxes. Every night, he's out with the lamp and the rifle. He gets through a truck a year, on average, because once he is on the trail of Charles James nothing gets in his way and the springs and wings take a considerable pasting as the result.

You might reasonably ask when the wild men eat and sleep if their days start at dawn and end in the wee small hours squeaking at foxes from behind a high powered light enhancing telescopic sight?

It's a reasonable question and to look at these keepers suggests that the answer is that they don't do much of either. They have a lean and hungry look, as the Bard has it. They seem not so much to wear their clothes as to inhabit them. Their eyes constantly dart here and there towards likely runs or earths or nests or lairs. They inhabit a front line where the enemy is everywhere and may attack at any time, from any direction, in any guise. But the wild men will be there, day or night with traps and guns and a ruthless determination to preserve their charges from the air or on the ground, fur or feather. It's a war. And that's all they know.

THE CELEBRITY GAME CHEF

'So what I'm going to do today is actually get myself a pheasant and then cook it for you absolutely fresh. From start to finish, as it were. From field to plate. How was that for sound, Colin?' Fine, fine. Crack on. 'So here I am on an actual shoot with my new friends. We've drawn for our positions and there are brushers or beaters in that wood over there who are going to drive the birds in our direction. At least, that's the plan. So here's hoping. Am I alright here, Colin? Can you get me in shot?' Yes, you're fine. We've even got your best side, such as it is. 'Oh, very funny, Colin.' Watch your front then, something seems to be happening. 'Aha! Now's my chance. Here comes a pheasant! Wow! Got it. That was fantastic. Did you get that, Colin?' 'Fraid not. Can you try to get it a bit earlier? Just about there; where that one is now? 'What one? Oh, I see. It's bit low though, isn't it?' It will look higher in the edit, believe me. Try this one. 'So here comes another. I think this one's mine. Bugger! Sorry, Colin. Never mind, here's another. Bugger! Of course, it's not easy getting your own food this way. That's what makes it so exciting. There! I've got one. Colin?' No, sorry. Right into the sun. Good angle of you though. 'Bloody hell, Colin, Can't we just CGI it into the edit?' Sorry. No can do. Too many phone-in scandals. Got to be TV verité these days, don'tcha know? A bit lower if you can, would be perfect. 'Okay. Okay. So here's my chance. Let's see if I can actually shoot myself a

pheasant. Bugger!' OI! COOKIE! KEEP YOUR *$*@*ING SHOT POINTED AT THE BIRDS, WILL YOU. WE'RE WORKING DOWN HERE!

'Sorry! Sorry! I told you that was too low, Colin. What's that going to do for my sporting credibility?' Don't worry, that we can edit out. I hope. Shall we move on? ...'

'...So here it is. My actual pheasant. It's beautiful, isn't it? Look at those glorious colours. It may seem a shame really but that is the harsh reality of life in the wild. And at least this bird has had a good life and free. Not locked up in some shed for its entire life. So now what we have to do is pluck it. You can remove the feathers a few at a time like this but it can take ages, so I'm going to show you another way that I have just been taught by my new country friends. You put the bird on its back like so. Then you place one foot on each wing – there and there – and then you just take a firm grip on the legs and ...nnnnnngggghhh!! ...voila!' JEEEZ! BLOODY HELL! UGH! YUK! OH MY GOD, WHATEVER IS ALL THAT?

'Wow! That's really something. Did you get that, Colin? Colin? Colin, what are you doing?' I'm just trying to get something out of the lens, as a matter of fact. 'Well, shouldn't you have done that before the shot? I mean, I believe that is the professional approach. What is it anyway?' I rather think it's pheasant liver. It's hard to tell what with all the blood. Did you have to do it that way?

'It's the authentic country way, Colin. And that's what we're all about, right? Authenticity? Yeah?' Of course, dear, of course. Did you have to be quite so, how shall I put this, athletically authentic?

'…So now I've cooked down the shallots, bunged in those gorgeous tatties, sautéed off the diced pheasant with plenty of seasoning and boshed in the red wine and the redcurrants. It's been on the stove now for – what? – forty-five minutes and it's smelling… mmmmmm! Pukka! Quite delicious. Pheasant au vin, done. So it's time to try it out on my new country chums. Here's Charlie. Charlie has been beating on the shoot here since the creation. Isn't that right, Charlie?' Ahhh! Urrgh! 'So there you go Charlie. What do you think of that? Colin, have you got the card for Charlie? Okay, Charlie, what's the verdict.'Ahhh!-Urrgh!-That-is-absolutely-deli-cious.-I-can't-think-when-I-have-tasted-pheas-ant-so-good.-Yum-yum-yum.Is-there-any-more? -Arrh!-Urrgh! 'Well done, Charlie. That's perfect. Colin?' Perfect. Got it. Thanks, Charlie. Well done. What's that, mate? Ahhh! I was jest explainin' to cookie here tha' if you's hung 'im fer a fortnight 'im might actually taste of summat, tha's al. Urrgh!

'That won't be in the edit, will it, Colin? Colin? Will it? Colin? Colin, are you all right? Colin? Can someone get Colin a glass of water please. Colin?

JEREMIAH

'Whit were ye thinkin', yer great lummox? Standing oot thir in the open wi' yer wee flag wavin' in the breeze? Did ye no see the birds driftin' awa' fra' ye? Did ye no think t'yersel' that wi' the wind the way it was ye might have scampered roond a wee bit? Ach! I might as weel be talking tae mysel'. Now don't you be givin' me looks like that, young Ben McNeill. Did I no' say t'ye that, if the wind picked up, ye was t'shift yersel' aboot to turrn them awa' frae the pines? Did I no? Aye, I did and well ye ken it. And did the breeze pick up? Aye. And where were ye, eh? Answer me that? It's a wonder the gennlemen go' any shootin' at all.

'And where were you, Jamie, when the birds were flushin? Aye, tha's as may be, lad, but were ye tappin' as I told ye to? Tap-tap-tap! It's no' a great challenge, even for such a turnip as yersel. All ye haff to do is keep tappin' awa' and the birds'll go where we want them an' no' leg it off doon the hedge like a scallywag wi' the polis on 'is erse.

'Ach weel. There were a few bangs fo' all that, so I may not be gettin' the dole for a wee while longer. Still, will ye no' try just a wee bit this drive to dae as I tell ye and no' go fiddle-faddlin' aboot like a lot of cackhanded teuchters.

'So, Jamie, I want ye t'mak ye way along the bottom hedge to where the burn joins the culvert. Ye ken wha' I'm sayin' tae ye noo, boy? Aye, work the dog as ye go but keep 'im close by, mind, an' don't let 'im ga fleein' aboot intae the wood or he'll have every bird there headin' back up the hill in a moment. Ye well ken how they're gey jittered a' this time of the season. Aye weel, mind ye do. If I see so much as a single cock runnin' toward me instead o' the Guns, ye'll ha' me to answer to, ye ken?

'Now, young Ben McNeill, will ye make ye way oot tae the left flank this time and keep yersel' well oot in the pasture where the birds'll see ye. If they're headin' doon the hill alreet, you leave 'em be but if they start to look oot tae the plantation beyond ye, up wi' yer flag an' turrn them back. An' use yer flag like a flagman this time, an' no like a tourist at the bluidy Edinburgh tattoo.

'Ha'e ye got it noo? Weel, here's hopin'. Now then, here come the Guns, so just you brace yersel's an' let me do the talkin'. Wi' luck they'll 'a had a wee dram an' no be too jaded by tha' last fiasco an' we'll ha' oor jobs an' hames yet. Good morning, sirs an' how are we the dee?'

'Ah, Hamish! Marvellous. Just marvellous. Super morning so far. Thanks awfully. That last drive was just a corker, wasn't it? I don't think they've gone that well yet this season, have they? Just superb. Everybody had lots to do and Mr Waverley here had an absolute blinder.'

'Nice tae see you again, Mr Waverley, sir. Och, so ye had a few over ye, did ye?'

'I should say so, Hamish. I don't think I've ever seen pheasants like that. I don't know how you do it. Really, I don't. Many, many thanks. I'll see you later, for sure. So long then, I can't wait to see what you've got in store for us next.'

'Very good, sir, we'll see if we can find anither or twa. Aye weel, lads, the Guns iss puttin' a brave face on it for sure. Let's all try not to make a dog's breakfast of the next one as weel. Tae yer places then an' wait for my whistle. We'll maybe salvage somethin' yet.'

THE GROUSE SHOOTER

There are shooters and there are grouse shooters. There are those who can knock down stratospheric pheasants all day and every day. There are some who can knock out a brace of partridges from every covey that flashes across the hedge. There are those who can kill four pigeons out of five while squatting on an oil drum in a ditch. They are all good shots. Some of them are great Shots. But grouse shooters are different. The grouse shooter is a Gun apart. By grouse shooter we do not mean all those who shoot grouse. Certainly not. Anyone can shoot grouse. Anyone with big money or good friends, that is. These are not grouse shooters however; they are people who shoot grouse.

True grouse shooters are altogether different. Some grouse shooters own grouse moors. This is certainly a start. If you own a grouse moor then you will cut your teeth on grouse. Every season – every grouse season when there are grouse, and on top moors there are always some grouse in a grouse season – the grouse shooter will be out there shooting grouse. Grouse shooters shoot grouse on their own moors. And then they shoot grouse on their neighbours' moors. And then they shoot grouse on their friends' moors. And then they shoot some more grouse. And then as the season progresses on those moors where there are still a lot of grouse the word goes out for the grouse shooters to come and help thin out the coveys before they pack because too many grouse at the end of the season can spell disaster the following year. So the grouse shooters gather.

They are Guns who can be relied upon to shoot grouse. Not the August cheepers but the back end grouse. Strong, fit and wary. Hurtling downwind across the heather on a brisk November breeze. With a bit of sleet in its teeth. This is where the grouse shooters who do not own moors begin to join the sport. They may be friends, some will be keepers, others will be highly regarded grouse Shots. What they will all be is capable of shooting grouse. Back-end grouse. Hard grouse. Tough grouse. Fast grouse. If grouse shooting is the hardest and best of shooting then back-end grouse is the hardest and best of grouse shooting. And there are not many shooters who can get into these teams with any regularity. But those who are bidden are the grouse shooters.

They don't look any different and they don't sound any different. They joke and josh and banter like any other group of Guns. But when they move into their butts they become grouse shooters. There to kill grouse.

Their guns are worn smooth with use. Their bags and belts are soft and loose to facilitate fast reloading. A couple of seconds is another covey and every covey is another chance and each chance is a brace or more in the heather. This is the way of the grouse shooter. Grouse shooters shoot fast and hard. Two or three cartridges

always in the left hand. A dozen or so more arranged on the edge of the butt. Speed loaders hung on the wall within easy reach. Everything focused, balanced, arranged, ready. Speed is important, concentration critical, accuracy para- mount. Grouse shooting is just shooting at grouse. But shooting grouse is an art which few can master and at which fewer still can excel. And those few are the grouse shooters. Altogether different.

SMALL PACKAGES

We all know how important it is to be polite and agreeable to the beaters and pickers-up on a shoot day. Our fun would be impossible without them and their efforts. So when you spot a small bundle of Barbour with its sleeves turned up and frog-eye wellies poking out of the bottom holding on to a lively looking Labrador with a keen eye one is always inclined to pass a word or two.

'Hello there. And what's your name then?'

'Thamantha.'

'And is this your doggie?'

'Yeth.'

'And what's his name?'

'Hith name'th Teal.'

'And have you been training him?'

'Yeth. He'th not a bad dog.'

'I'm sure he'th…sorry… he's a very good dog. Perhaps we can get a pheazzie for him this drive.'

'That'th what we're here for, I thuppose.'

'Well, maybe I'll see you later then.'

'Thure. Good luck.'

And after the drive, as you wander back to look for that longish bird that your conscience tells you that you should search for despite it having been little more than tickled, there she is again but now with a brace of birds slung over her shoulder.

'You've got a couple then, have you?'

'Yeth.'

'And did Teal pick them up for you?'

'Yeth. He'th not a bad dog.'

'Good for him. And did you happen to see a cock bird go back a ways with a bit of a leg down, by any chance?'

'Yeth. You nearly mithed it. I wath going to get him now.'

'Jolly good.'

'Teal! Giddout!'

And the lively Labrador with the keen eye takes off like a sleek black missile. At the fence he pauses. 'Peep! Teal! Giddover!' And he's over and gone and covers the next hundred metres in the blink of an eye. 'Peep! Pee-pip!' Teal casts back and forth and then dashes into a nearby hedge. 'He'th on it now. It'th a wunner.' Teal emerges from the hedge with a lively looking cock. 'Pip-pip! Pip-pip!' and he's back over the fence at full tilt in a flash and offering it up from a sitting position before you can say field trial championship material. 'That'th a good boy.' Samantha gives the cock a whack with her stick and adds it to the sling over her shoulder.

The head keeper ambles past with a handful of birds. 'Take those for you, Sam, shall I? How'd it go at the Spillers then?'

'Thecond to Halthtead again. But I reckon we'll 'ave 'im by next theason if we keep at it. But we only need one more plathe to qualify for the European Juniorth.'

And you called him a doggie. On a good day the earth might open up and swallow you.

THE GROUSE MOOR OWNER

When you have had a bit of success in life, actually when you have had a good deal of success in life, in fact, if we are brutally honest, when you have cleaned up big time in life – and by your own sweat and tears, it might be added, not by some mega-rollover-Euro-jackpot lottery win though we are talking those sorts of numbers, the sort with seven or more zeros on the end – then it becomes a chap to rein back, whisper a prayer of thanks to whatever gods he believes in, review the old work–life balance and decide that now would be a good time to turn his mind to spending a bit of quality time with the family and perhaps indulging himself somewhat and, in short, to focus rather less on the accumulation of ludicrous riches and somewhat more on the spending side of the equation. Some might opt for houses here and there. As it might be, London, New York, Cap Ferrat and, say, Mexico. Others might contemplate a small island in the West Indies or the tropics or, maybe, a not so small one in the current bargain basement, the Aegean. Or it might be a yacht. Or a football club. A polo team. A motor racing team. Or a clutch of Impressionists. Something that says a bit about a chap. A man of taste, discretion and simply colossal amounts of boodle.

Or it might be a grouse moor. Grouse moors are rare. There aren't very many of them. They don't come onto the market terribly often and they sure as hell aren't making any more of them.

So a grouse moor ticks all the boxes. It is rare, expensive, cannot be replaced by a new model, will be an agreeable management project much like an allotment on a grand scale, has a house attached, rampant exclusivity and makes a properly discreet statement. And it will be fun.

So he signs on the dotted line and that's when the dream begins to fray at the edges. First, the thing needs improving. 'Ah, well, ye see, Surr, the previous owner never really took as much interest in it as he should. But surely ye'll be wanting to do right by the auld place?'

So more drains need to go in and access roads are a must and the butts all need replacing and the bothy is a disgrace. But the place is littered with SSSIs, AOONIs, internationally recognised breeding colonies of things you've never heard of and there is a blizzard of paperwork to be ploughed through before he can set foot on the place let alone start digging holes in it. The drains are a tenner a metre and the road is twice that without even a surface on it but these sums are petty cash compared to the lawyers' bills to fend off the objections of battalions of government, non-government, European and self-appointed busybodies, prodnoses and clipboard wranglers who appear from nowhere and cluster about the place like ticks on a dog.

You would at least think that the keepers would be on his side but his every suggestion for positioning this or proposing that are met with a pursed lip and a raised eyebrow.

'Weeeell, ye see, Surr, that would work fine on most moors. Indeed, it would be grand for most moors but, ye see, just here the prevailing wind-the ground-the burn-the heather-the birds-the slope-the air temperature-the ground temperature-the microclimate is ever so slightly different. And so your idea – exciting and innovative as it undootedly is, Surr – is completely unsuitable and out of the question.'

And all this is before the grouse themselves chip in by periodically dying in droves for no particularly good reason despite everyone's best – and expensive – efforts.

And so it is that rather than the owner taking over the moor, the moor gradually absorbs the owner; and while his ambitions may be frustrated and his massive fortune substantially diminished, every now and again there will be a good season and he will entertain his friends – of which there will be many – to glorious days of glorious sport and, Lo, truly his cup runneth over and his spirits shall soar to the very skies and he shall be as a prince among men and shall know happiness beyond price.

Which is just as well really, when you consider the price.

THE REACHER

It's not as if he is actually a bad shot. He could hit things. He can hit things. From time to time. What he is, though, is slow. Too slow. He stands at his peg with his gun cradled in his elbow. Now this is not a bad thing. It's what they describe in the books as being the proper and appropriate – and safe – way to wait for a pheasant. And it is. On a grand shoot where the pheasants get up simply miles away and come rocketing and gliding towards the line at full speed in open sky to offer that most challenging of targets: the curling, gliding bird.

This is not, however, the grandest of shoots. It's not a bad shoot. Actually, it's not a bad shoot at all. It's quite a good shoot, really, but it is not grand. And the pheasants are likely to emerge from the copse at only a little remove and clatter over the shelter belt just in front of him. And they will be going a bit because the wind will be behind them. That is why the keeper drives them this way. This is why they do this drive when the wind is in this direction. This is how to make the best of the resources available on a good, rather than a great, shoot. But he hasn't clocked this. Because his mind is elsewhere. Perhaps still at work. Maybe on the lissome lady beside whom he sat at dinner last evening and with whom he thinks that he was making pretty good progress. Or possibly on the mysteries of quantum physics. The thing he is not thinking about is what he is going to do when the pheasants arrive.

And as the consequence when the pheasant does arrive he is surprised. Startled. Discombobulated. His head comes up as if the pheasant is the last thing he was expecting. Which it was. The gun is disentangled from the elbow – eventually – and, in due season, the first barrel is duly discharged. And duly whistles past the pheasant's tail some several feet behind.

But this is where the Reacher comes into his own. For now he looks up further as the pheasant flies over his head as if confused. And then he slowly turns and watches its departure into the distance as if expecting it, at any moment, to suffer a fatal heart attack and collapse onto the plough.

Maybe not. But he's sure he can still reach it. And then he takes careful aim, squinting carefully along the barrels, tongue poking out of the corner of his mouth and, in due season, duly discharges the second barrel. Which catches the pheasant squarely in the arse and blows out a few feathers. And then he watches for a bit longer as it glides away. Still banking on that heart attack to finish the job at any moment.

And, in the distance, a picker up squints into the sun as the pheasant drops a leg and sets its wings. He knows the Reacher. And he knows that the Reacher will collar him in two drives time and ask whether he has retrieved that 'hard hit cock from the shelter belt that should be dead on its back, I reckon.' The dog is already on the line but it will be a sprint to the finish because the Reacher's birds are usually in reasonable fettle. Sore of arse but fleet of foot.

Trouble is, he can reach them. Just.

THE BEATKEEPER

He's young and he's keen, and he's fresh and he's nice. He's shockingly enthusiastic about the whole thing, and making a decent fist of not looking too nervous. The problem is that the rest of us are old, jaded, cynical and half knackered to boot. But then life was ever thus. It's the first time through on the beat and while the host has not chanced his arm by asking the First XI, the young keeper can't yet tell the difference. The head keeper is floating around somewhere in the background pretending to be a beater, and everyone is being solicitous, which makes the poor young man more nervous than ever. You tell him not to worry and everything will be fine, but all he hears is 'Screw today up and you'll never work in this county again.'

He looks a little uncomfortable in his new estate tweed, as well he might, for anyone familiar with the cloth will tell him that chucking it into the river for a day or two is about the only way to render it wearable for the first ten years or so. His face and his wellies are scrubbed with equal ferocity so that he shines at both ends. He has a spaniel, which is as young and quite as nervous about proceedings as he is, attached to a piece of rope. The fact that the spaniel is bouncing round his ankles in a frenetic attempt to trip him and strangle itself into the bargain does little for the equilibrium of either.

The first drive is a modest success. Thus encouraged the beatkeeper attempts a dramatic new departure in the big wood by reversing the drive in the middle in order to take account of a sudden windshift. As a consequence the beaters end up going in one direction and the birds in quite another. At the end of the drive therefore the birds have seen no beaters, the Guns have seen not a feather of the birds and the beaters are nowhere to be seen. Still, it was a brave try. Innovative. Intelligent. Creative. Everything they taught at college. It just also happened to be wrong. In a sterling bid for redemption the next drive is undertaken at a snail's pace in order that not a bird is overlooked. This results in the Guns waiting 40 minutes for the first bird to appear, and about ten seconds for the next several hundred. At which point the beatkeeper abandons all his carefully laid plans, and empties his mind of everything except his imminent dismissal at the end of the day. He even lets the bonkers spaniel off the lead. The next several drives are a perfect example of what happens when nothing matters any more. The beaters enjoy themselves, the birds fly high, wide and handsome and the visiting Guns have a ball.

They are free at the end of the day with their congratulations and with generous tips. As the beatkeeper is dogging in his birds and checking his feed rides that evening, the host and his headkeeper are comparing notes over a glass. 'I remember our first day together,' says the one. 'Well, whose idea was it to face the Guns that way in the first place?' says the other.

Life was ever thus.

LESS IS THE NEW MORE

Remember yuppies? They were very big in the '80s. City types. Big suits, big hair and a car with a great big wing on the back. Remember them? Then they morphed into something else. They didn't go away exactly but they became something else. And by the time we got to the millennium they were middle-aged. Middle-aged, middle class and very, very rich. New Labour just loved them. Less big suits now than sharp. I mean exquisitely cut. Discreet, even. And they were still in the City. Only now they weren't just jobbing and broking and making the coffee; they were running the place. And the money. Boy, oh boy, the money just rolled in. Like a tide. Like a tidal wave. Every twelve months another cataract of cash. And then they ran it into a wall.

And so things have had to change. Fortunately, the farm is safe. Well, one says the farm. Actually, it's the weekend house. Well, it was the weekend house but now that there is no week in the City in between weekends it is just referred to as the farm. Even though there is no farming as such. There is a certain amount of grass cutting and there are Annabel's horses, of course, and there is a tractor – somewhere about – but that was only really for show. And to demonstrate to the Defra box tickers that it was a proper working farm to keep the Stewardship cheques rolling in.

There are a few pheasants about the place.

And so, from time to time, he invites some of the chaps round to have a lash at them. In a sort of postmodern ironic way. Actually in a sort of postmodern financial meltdown way, ironically, if we are going to be completely accurate.

In the glory days they would be shooting three days a week. On the firm. In those days shooting was the big corporate hostility thing. Bags went up and up. Two-fifty here. Three hundred there. Four. Five. A day here. Two days there. This house, that manor, his hall, their castle. Let it be known about the brokerage houses that you enjoyed a bit of a bang at the longtails and the invites simply rolled in. Like a tide. Oops, have we been here before?

Well, now the tide's gone out and as it happens a lot of chaps were skinny dipping. Well, perhaps not skinny exactly. The farm is safe, after all. And the flat. And the villa, for that matter. And the kids won't have to leave school or anything like that. I mean, it's not their money that has been poured down the drain, is it? But economies must be made. Belts tightened. It's expected.

So the five hundred bird days are off and instead they chase a handful of pheasants round each other's farms. Ironically, obviously. Although, secretly, they quite like it. Turns out that it's the company and the crack, and not the bag, after all, that makes for a jolly shooting day. Which is, if you like, the final irony.

THE YOUNG DOG

'Yes, well she's only young but we have high hopes for her. Oh, absolutely, her pedigree is littered with champions. So it should be the amount I shelled out. And I sent her off to a top trainer for three months. And that wasn't cheap either, I can tell you. So, yes, you could say that she represents a bit of an investment. Ha! Ha! No, I haven't taken her out before. But there must be a first time for everything, what?'

And so it goes.

At the peg he takes no chances. The young dog is not screwed into the sod with a great tether like a bad dog would be because, after all, expectations are high what with her pedigree and her training and the considerable investment and what have you. Oh yes, expectations are high. Optimism is a precondition to having a young dog. Where would we be otherwise? But what with the pedigree and the training and the considerable investment if optimism isn't justified, what is? Experience is nothing where a young dog is concerned. Hope is everything.

And during the drive the young dog sits appropriately quiet and virtuous and doesn't whine or cry or pull. Even when a bird falls only a tug and a leap and a bound away the young dog stays calm. Alert and attentive, for sure, but calm. Well, calmish. There is a quiver in the haunches and the young dog's eyes are alight with expectation. Her moment will come.

And as the horn goes to mark the end of the drive, the young dog's owner does the sensible thing and makes the young dog stay while he picks up the nearby birds which are, after all, only a tug and a leap and a bound away and which are an unnecessary distraction for a young dog, are they not? What a young dog needs is a properly dead bird, at a little remove, but in open view where performance can be monitored, isn't it? So the nearest birds are cleared and when there is just the perfect novice retrieve waiting a few tens of yards away the leash is finally removed. But there is no riot and rush. Certainly not. The young dog is properly settled. 'Wait. Wait. Wait. Steady. Steady.' One-two-three-four-five-six-seven-eight-nine-ten. 'Hie lost then!' and the young dog is away like a flash across the sward. Straight to the point of fall. Flat out. A pause. Sorry, a check. A sniff here at the scattered feathers. 'Hie lost! Gid'on!'

She looks back. She looks at the cock lying immobile on the pasture. A leap and a bound and she's there. 'Bring it on then, girl!' The young dog takes a few moments to scoop the bird firmly into her jaws. 'Bring it on then!'

And the young dog looks back. And calculates. And computes. He'll never get here in time. Not in his condition.

And up into the air goes the cock. And down. And up and down. And she pounces on it again, pushing it this way with her paws and that. For all the world as if she is giving the damn thing CPR. 'Bring it on then!' There is a new note in his voice now. And optimism isn't really it. The young dog picks the cock up again. Shakes it this way and that. Resettles it in her mouth once more. And she's off. Away towards the distant wood and the start of the next drive. 'PEEEEEEEPPPP!' She checks. Looks. 'PEEEEEPPPP!' Please. Please. Oh, please. Shake. Toss. Balance on the nose. Shake. Catch. 'PEEEEEEP!' And here she comes. Hurrah! Just like the field trial champion she should be, will be, is.

And straight past the master without even a pause and away. One circle, two circles, three. 'Loog ad me, Dad! Loog ad me! I'be gorra peasant! Loog ad me!' And she takes it to the next Gun. And his neighbour. And the beaters. And the keeper. And the host. 'Loog, mate, I'be goddun!' But will she share it? That's the question isn't it? 'NOOOOOOO! NOOOO WAAAAYYY! I'BE GODDA PEASANT! LOOG-ADMEEE!' And so it goes. And optimism goes with it. And brings experience. That's a young dog for you.

SON OF A GUN

Do you remember the Young Gun? Thirteen or so? Wedged into the line with his new 20 bore between Uncle Jack and his mate Pongo for discreet supervision? Pink of cheek and bursting with pride at the felling of his first pheasant in grown up company at the Boxing Day shoot? Remember him?

Well, that was nine years ago would you believe? So that when his Dad calls to say that he can't make it on Saturday and would it be alright if he sends the boy along to carry his gun in his stead obviously you agree.

Except that what turns up is not the fresh-faced child of distant memory bursting with excitement and throbbing with nerves at his first day in the line. What uncoils itself from behind the wheel of the familiar farm Land Rover that his father usually turns up in is now two yards and more of muscular manhood which has the appearance of being almost as broad as it is long. The hair is still blond but is no longer cut in a school pudding basin but flops here and there in errant style. The face is recognisable but more as the consequence of its similarity to how his father looked when you first met him, what, thirty years gone? Gone too is the reedy treble to be replaced by a gravelly bass that booms good morning and is backed up by a handshake that feels like it has agricultural hydraulics somewhere in the forearm.

The new Barbour and Hunters of yore are gone too and now a well used Schoffel and worn Aigles are pulled from the back of the truck. Cartridges are no longer pushed one by one from a fresh box into the loops of a still stiff Christmas belt but are stuffed into a stained bag from a broken case of 250. 'Still got your old twenty, then?' you wonder as he takes a leather sleeve from the passenger side of the Defender. 'Actually, no,' he replies, 'I still use a twenty but I traded in the side-by-side for one of these.' And he unzips the slip and draws forth an elegant, indeed exquisite, Italian O/U sidelock. 'Dad went a bit mental when I first got it, of course. Said it wasn't the thing at all but judging by the amount of use it seems to get when I'm away at uni, he seems to have come round to it, I imagine. Actually I think he'd quite like one himself but he just can't admit that they're easier to shoot with.'

Whether they are easier to shoot with or not may be a moot point but what is certain is that he shoots with it very well. Very well indeed. Actually, astonishingly well. He's not showy and he does not obliterate everything that comes near him. Quite the reverse, in fact. Which makes it all the more obvious. He waits at his peg with the little gun resting on his shoulder enveloped in a meaty fist and when the birds begin to move he simply reaches out and takes one here and perhaps another there. Except that they are not simply there and here, if you see what I mean, they are rather right over there and right over here. Miles away. Some are high and some are long; but they are all without exception impressive. And he doesn't just shoot them either. He really kills them, stone dead.

And, of course, he's charming and diffident and polite and funny into the bargain just like his father. He's a real son of a Gun.

THE SPORTING DIVORCEE

It is said that a woman in possession of a small fortune must know a good lawyer. And it is certainly true of Camilla. Actually she must know a really good lawyer because her fortune is considerable. The first divorce saw her comfortably off but the second was a blinder. Not that it was her intention in either case, or indeed her fault. Camilla is probably lucky at cards too because she has proved to be singularly unlucky in love. At least if your first husband cuts and runs within a few months of your honeymoon, being followed by your second setting up home with his chauffeur after twenty years of apparent marital contentment – if not exactly bliss, it must be said – is anything to go by.

Still, Camilla is a trouper and she soldiers on. Cushioned admittedly by that considerable fortune. She divides the bulk of her time between her town house in SW3 and her delirious villa in Umbria but the shooting season sees her much on the road between the commodious country homes of her many friends for the shooting.

She came to the sport through her first husband, behind whom she dutifully stood for the only season that they were together. During her second lap round the block as a wife and then mother she again stood dutifully behind her spouse at many shoots through many seasons. It was only when the boys were in their early teens and she was driving them hither and yon to boys' shoots up and down the country

that Camilla decided it was time to get more actively involved in order that she could advise – and where necessary correct – them in relation to their equipment, their technique and, most importantly, their behaviour.

So she took herself off to one of the London shooting schools where she found a gentle and agreeable coach who taught her the basics. And seeing a real talent for the whole undertaking in Camilla he went on to coach her further in more advanced techniques and how to cope with tricky targets and the truly marginal bird which distinguishes the top end Gun from the journeyman shooter. And Camilla worked diligently and hard and well and quickly developed into a really stylish and accomplished Shot. In addition to which she found that she absolutely loved it to bits.

And as a really stylish and accomplished Shot as well as being an agreeable companion and a woman in possession of a considerable fortune and easy on the eye into the bargain she found herself with no shortage of invitations which she reciprocates from time to time by taking days here and there on top estates and inviting her many shooting friends to test their mettle against the best birds the finest keepers in the kingdom can put over them.

And who knows what the future will bring? The shooting field is much populated, after all, by chaps who have no inclination to cohabit with their drivers, and some of them are even single, and a woman who is a really stylish and accomplished Shot as well as being easy on the eye and in possession of a considerable fortune to boot can afford to pick and choose and to browse to her heart's content. So it might even be that Camilla's luck will change. And why not?

THE HOOVER

There comes a moment at this time of the year, when, as it might be, you are shooting partridges, that you find yourself plodding back and forth about a field of stubble turnips or perhaps sugar beet or plough or even just a wheat stubble in pursuit of a downed bird that you marked exactly but which now doesn't seem to be where you thought it was or should have been. There are dogs running about to be sure but they are not yours and they seem to be busy enough in any event picking up their own birds and not to have any interest in yours particularly. Or perhaps they have already picked up yours and yet you cannot be sure. There are pickers-up in the distance too but they are focusing on those birds that flew on to fall well back from the line of Guns and who are courteously allowing the Guns' dogs to rampage about unhindered nearer to the pegs and too far away to be of much immediate help.

It's frustrating. You know it's here somewhere and yet it has vanished utterly. And then you hear your host saying, 'Guns this way please. We must get on if we want to get two more in before lunch.' And you don't want to leave a marked bird unfound. It's not fair; it's not sporting; and it's not done, is it? So you say to your host, don't you, 'I've got one down hereabouts but I'm damned if I can find it but I'm sure it's dead.' And your host says, doesn't he, 'Not to worry. We're not leaving it. The Hoover will be coming through after us. Come on.'

And you look into the distance and there is the reassuring sight of the Hoover making his way down the lane and turning in at the gate.

He has an elderly van. Usually an old Escort van or perhaps an Astra. Probably it's a singularly inappropriate colour. Yellow. Or lime green. Sometimes both where a panel has been replaced here or there with a salvage job. And as he opens the back there is a pause and then with a snap of the fingers there issues forth a veritable cascade of spaniels.

They do not scamper and riot though. They assemble about his heels in a joyous gaggle; each gazing up at the Hoover with a silent entreaty to be allowed to get about their business. And as the Guns' wagon pulls out of the same gate the Hoover says quietly, 'Giddon then, Teal. Giddout, Tern. Steady, Fern. Giddon, Sedge. Go on then, Fern. Just you wait, Drake. Out, Tarn. On you go now, Drake.'

And the tumbling horde set off in a glorious tide of springing, bouncing dogginess doing what comes naturally to a bunch of Springers. And they pick a bird here or as it might be a runner there and either is instantly brought to hand and offered up to the Hoover who receives it with a word of praise before unleashing the tide once more. And in the ten minutes after the Guns have left the Hoover has accumulated an additional couple of handfuls of game. Some the Guns couldn't find, some they didn't even know they were looking for.

And the keeper knows that with the Hoover's help he'll make the bag. And the host knows that he will get all the drives in he needs and wants. And you know that the bird you marked down diligently but which wasn't there when you looked for it will be Hoovered up in due course and your conscience can rest easy therefore. Aye, he's a reassuring sight, the Hoover.

ALL DOWNHILL FROM HERE

We all know about highland stalkers. We all know highland stalkers. Those lean and wiry men, Hamish perhaps, or Archie, who lope easily up vertiginous slopes without, apparently, ever needing to breathe or breaking into any kind of sweat. And with a rifle on their back into the bargain. They only stop to spy the hillside opposite and suck their teeth and say, 'Aye. There's beasts in the corrie the dee. We'll hie oop and roond an' drop doon on them frae the peak. Aye. Tha'll serve.' And he hefts the rifle and sets off again at the same steady, relentless pace.

Oh, we know stalkers, alright.

But what of the client? The Rifle? The chap behind the trigger when the moment finally comes?

The Rifle is the bloke lying in the heather with sweat flooding from every pore. His face is puce, his breathing laboured and the world is dancing before his bulging eyes. With a shaking hand he lifts the binoculars and attempts to focus on the opposite slope, but with his heaving chest it is almost impossible to see anything through the red haze let alone to see any deer. All he can see – or more particularly feel – is the cloud of midges that surrounds his perspiration-drenched brow and dives in from time to time to sip at his salty sweat and leave a stinging kiss in return.

And this is supposed to be a holiday. Vacation; rest and recreation. Where does a first division route march, flat out, up a cliff face come into that equation, he'd like to know?

It seemed so attractive in the brochure. Turretted lodge, cook and bottlewasher, loch before and river behind, some mature forestry and the open hill beyond. Opportunities for every kind of sport for a sporting gentleman. And being a sporting gentleman he duly signed on the dotted line.

And having dipped a fly in the loch and a lure in the river, and having strolled in the mature forestry, what does a sporting chap do but whistle up the stalker and embark upon the pursuit of a mighty monarch o' the glen?

And did he practise for this expedition? Did he train? Did he buggery. Well, he did slip from his dusty stool in the counting house on a couple of evenings last week and spend half an hour on the treadmill. Not on its harshest setting, obviously. Well, if he's honest, he did put it on the hardest setting to begin with, but since the pedals didn't seem to work very well – or indeed at all – when cranked up to the max, he turned it down again. And so now he is lugging his portly frame, complete with a magnificent feast from last night and a full English this morning served up by the cook and bottlewasher, up the north-west face of the Eiger behind a dour Scot who is manifestly the offspring of a ghastly accident between a Himalayan Sherpa and a mountain goat.

When – if – he ever makes it to the point of

discharge and the said dour Scot hauls him bodily up the last slope to the crest and plonks him behind the telescopic sight with the curt instruction to 'Tak the wee staggie tae the left. Wi' the spiky top on 'im,' he will look frantically through the lens for anything resembling a deer until Archie – or perhaps Hamish – shoves the barrel round until the requisite beast some few tens of yards off fills the 'scope in all his monarchy glory. Then he will attempt to slow his pounding heart, hold his labouring breath, ignore the savagery of the blasted midges and try not to yank the trigger and blow the whole painful and strenuous effort to the four winds.

And finally he squeezes and squeezes and squeezes and …BOOMMPHH! The gun bucks, his hat falls over his eyes as he slides back down the slope and the 'scope fills with sky.

'Aye,' says Hamish – or perhaps Archie – 'he's doon.'

And so eventually will be the Rifle, God and pulmonary crises permitting. After all, it's all downhill from here.

THE CARTRIDGE CADGER

'I say, you couldn't help me out with a handful of shells, could you? I seem to have left my bag in the gun bus.' And before you really know what you are doing you shove a hand in your bag – or as it might be your pocket – and pass him a couple of handfuls. 'Thanks awfully. I'll get some back to you at elevenses, OK?' Yes. Fine. Whatever. Whenever. And, of course, come elevenses, or perhaps lunch, he doesn't and they don't. In fact, he's just in the process of tapping someone else. 'Ooh-er, I seem to be headed for the pound seat and I've only got a few squibs in my pocket. I couldn't grab a few off you, could I? I'll see you right before the next drive.' But, as usual, the walk to the next drive finds him somewhere else. And heaven forbid that you find yourselves anywhere near water or waterfowl. 'Non-toxics? Cripes! I've got a couple in my belt. Never travel without them but if we're going to see more than a moorhen I'll be buggered. You haven't got a few spare have you? You're a love. I'll catch up with you later. I'm sure there's a box in the car.' In the car, in the bag, in the wagon. In your dreams. Come the moment and he's gone like the morning mist.

Someone should say something but everyone is, naturally, far too nice. And too generous. 'Not to worry.' 'Anytime.' 'That's all right.' And by the time he's touched everyone in the line for a handful, the crafty tyke is two boxes to the good and there is about as much chance of them coming back as there is of seeing the change off an MP.

How many would you have to lose before you mentioned it? Exactly. Anything less than a full box and we all tend to grin and bear it. Which is why his bag is always half full with a motley collection of blagged bullets and all of ours are half empty.

There is a solution, of course. Indeed, there are solutions. The first and most obvious is to give him the turnabout and tell him to bog off. Time was that anyone running out of ammunition was sent home forthwith on the firm understanding that he'd had all the fun he was expecting and deserved no more. Them were days. Or you could just carry what you need and leave your own bag behind and assert firmly that you have no spares. Best of all, avoid 12 bores and 20 bores like the plague. Sixteens are uncommon. Twenty-eights rare and a 32 bore will flummox even the most diligent scrounger. Or you can palm him off with a black powder banger. If the shock when it goes off doesn't give him a heart attack the cleaning afterwards certainly will. Or you can tot them all up between you over the course of the season and present him with a joint invoice at the end of the last day. That should get the point across.

On the other hand, it might not, because the cartridge cadger tends to have the hide of your average rhino. Still, you never know.

FRUIT OF THE HEDGE

He is hunched. For all the world like an old rook. He stands on his peg and his dog lies obediently at his feet. But he is oblivious. The gun hangs unsleeved on his shoulder. In the distance the beaters are tap-tap-tapping through the covert. Pheasants begin to move, raucous, through the undergrowth and start to clatter into the air. But he is unmoved. Hands extended to the bottom of his jacket he stares transfixed as if in solemn contemplation. Almost as if in prayer. Not though to the heavens but to some lower deity. As if to the very earth itself. And yet it is not a prayer – unless it is a deep and abiding wish that he had remembered his glasses this morning so that he could see what, exactly, it is that Alice – his PA – is trying to remind him of. Or perhaps alert him to. Or warn him. Or just tell him. Perhaps where his glasses are. Or where he is supposed to be. Or when.

And as the first of the birds begin to stream across his airspace he turns this way and that the better to catch the sun to illuminate the screen or perhaps the shade to highlight the distant letters. Finally he loses patience, removes the earmuffs and jabs the redial button.

This is the Blackberry man. Up to the minute, cutting edge, on the case, never out of touch, constantly available, only ever an e-mail away. As long, that is, as he has his glasses with him. Otherwise the tiny screen is merely a frustrating blur at waist height. Enticing, alluring, tempting, seething with the promise of vital information were it not encrypted by hyperopia. That's longsightedness to you and me but hyperopia to him because he has wireless connectivity and so can check the formal classification in an instant. If only he could stretch his arms a little further.

'Hello, Alice. Alice? Hello? Alice? Hello? Hello? Alice. Oh hi! You mailed me? Yes, I got it but I can't make it out. No, I'm shooting. Well, I'm not actually shooting because I'm talking to you, aren't I? So what is it? Well, obviously I am here. I just said so, didn't I?'

'Over! Over!' the beaters cry, as he stamps back and forth, kicking petulantly at a mole-hill. As if waking from a trance he looks up and seems to notice only now that there are pheasants filling the air over his head. With the machine still clamped to his ear he shrugs the slip from his shoulder and begins to fumble at the buckle one handed.

'Well, what did it say, then? Well, open the attachment, please.' With the gun now under his one free arm he is trying to find some cartridges single-handed from the cartridge belt which is buried under several layers of jacket. 'You're breaking up. YOU'RE BREAKING UP! DAMMIT. DAMMIT. DAMMIT. YOU'RE BREAKING.... No, sorry, not you. You were breaking up, sorry. No, I wasn't shouting at you. OK, so what is it? Directions to where? Alice, just hold on, will you?' With the Blackberry now clamped between stock and ear he attempts to shoot a

pheasant. The pheasant is, needless to say, unaffected by the blast but the silver toy slips from its position and plummets to the dewy sward below. 'SHIT!!' he reaches down, and in so doing jams his muzzles into the molehill as aforesaid. 'Double shit!' he says, wiping the thing against his breast. 'So what does it say, please, Alice?' He is now looking down the barrels and shaking them back and forth in an attempt to dislodge the mud that now blocks them. 'Alice, dearheart, I'm already here. I've been here before. Remember? I know the way. Yes, well it was very kind of you. Thank you. But I am here. Ok. Bye, love.'

But he is not really here. Any more than he is there, either. He is in limbo somewhere in between. On the fence perhaps. Or in the hedge. He is a Blackberry, after all.

FAIR MAIDEN

Jo is nineteen and in the midst of her gap
year. She's down for Exeter come the
Autumn – law, actually, so there – not just a
pretty face then. Though it is a pretty face.
Of course it is. And lissome besides. Well,
she's nineteen, isn't she?

Lissome goes with the territory. Mane
of tousled locks, smattering of freck-
les and despite the miserable spring
there is still the hint of a tan. That
would be the leftovers of a ski season
chalet-bunnying in Chamonix topped up in
the garden with such sunshine as there has been
so far this summer. That and riding out morning
and evenings at home to keep the horses fit.

There is a last trip to parts foreign scheduled
for the back end of summer before Uni begins.
Hong Kong, Vietnam and down to Oz for a
couple of months. So there is an urgent need to
top up financially before then. She's done an
internship at one of the top London law firms
which was lucrative enough but if Down Under
is to be more fun than toil then any earner is
grist to her mill, and so three days flouncing in
front of a stand at the Game Fair, cash in hand,
is a gimme. And she gets to keep the clothes
into the bargain.

For real, it's a doddle. Jo would be going to the Fair anyway. It's been a family outing for, like, forever. She remembers being carried around on Dad's shoulders when she was little more than a toddler, running into the ring to meet the hounds and posing for a picture with a falcon on her wrist.

And, like, everyone, will be there. Although she has some friends who are town based – Jo has friends everywhere, after all, and is quite as at home in Chelsea as Cheltenham – the Game Fair is pretty much on the social circuit. Aintree, Cheltenham, Badminton, Henley, Wimbledon, the Game Fair, Burghley. It's a social roll call and all the bright young things participate.

Picnics and parties; parties and picnics. A kiss for luck and we're on our way. It worked for Miss Joan Hunter Dunn and it works for Jo today. And Caro and Libby and Flavia and Charlie and Ed and Marco.

But won't it be difficult to be working at the Fair when everyone else is partying?

Well, no. For one thing there is a whole gang who have signed on for the three days. Claire and Sal and Ally are waitressing in the Members, and Tim and Andy are behind the bar – so that's free drinks all round for starters. A bunch of other girls and boys will be variously employed about the show in diverse capacities – the capacity of the young to turn a buck in these straitened times is much underrated – and so there will be considerable partying every night after the public have left the show in the evening. And everyone gets in for free. There will be much passing of staff badges back and forth through the fence for those who haven't the wherewithal for a Member's ticket.

So, lissome and lovely, carefree at summer party central, and paid for the whole weekend to walk about enjoying the Fair – looking lissome and lovely and carefree – in free clothes. And then off to Honkers.

Kid's got it made. Watch her and weep.

THE BATTLE BUS

It may be a Range Rover, or a Shogun or some other four-wheel drive. Or it might be a saloon of some description. The make and model is of little import. What is sure is that it does a lot of miles. It will be stained therefore with the salt and grit that are spread on the roads, with any luck, at this time of year. Streaked from the wind and rain and snow and mud. Because he does a lot of miles. From one end of the country to the other and back again. Crossing and re-crossing county after county. Hampshire today, Shropshire tomorrow, Wiltshire Friday.

And not just counties either but countries. As it might be Scotland on Monday, Wales on Wednesday and the weekend down in the west country. Then Yorkshire, the east coast and Norfolk next week with a pause at home in between for a bit of a launder, recognise the family and to drop off the bootful of game garnered after the battues of the past few days and to pick up a couple more slabs of shells for the stands to come. He is the travelling Gun. In the battle bus. On the road again.

The front end of what he refers to, universally, as 'The truck' is largely business. There is a laptop, Blackberry, the i-phone – maybe more than one – and a dictaphone and the MP3; with a tangle of chargers trailing from the dash. There are files and memo pads and Post-its and pens heaped on the passenger seat. There is a dark suit hanging from the grab handle and a bag of assorted shirts in the footwell. It is a model of the mobile office. Anything can be done from here. Anyone can be contacted. Meetings arranged. Clients visited and investors met. Research analysed. Figures considered. Agreements negotiated. Settlements arrived at. Cases pursued. Deals done. Then back on the road. There is a PA somewhere. Somewhere else. To follow up. To diarise. There are associates to confirm, follow up, follow through and to finish. This is just the sharp end.

The back, however is all sport. There are gun cases and sleeves and cartridge bags and boots. There are several slabs of cartridges in assorted calibres and sizes. There are coats and breeches and hats. Another bag with stockings and garters and scarves and gloves. There may even be a dog. Or two. And their beds and blankets and bags of food. Leads and towels and water bowls. And the pheasants from yesterday and the day before and a few feathers still lying about from the week before.

Some of the shoots will be front end related. Business. There will be selected clients, coleagues, prospects. A lot of goodwill and a lot of deals can be done between drives or over a decent lunch. Others will be purely social. Old mates, family and friends. The wife and veg. might even turn out from time to time though they will come from home and when the time comes to leave they will return there. While he goes back on the road once more. To the next meeting, the next shoot, the next stand. He is the wandering Gun. Back in the battle bus. On the road again.

THE HISTORIAN

It starts as you are picking up your birds after the first drive. Your gun is tucked under your arm as you gather a cock here and a hen there. Your neighbour wanders over. 'Pretty gun you've got there,' he says, 'What is it, by the way?'

'Er, it's a Potter, actually.'

And so it begins.

'Ah,' he says, 'John Potter. John Young Potter. Of King's Lynn, as I recall. Indentured as an apprentice to the great Joseph Manton. Well, not the man himself, obviously, but in his factory. And then did a stint at Hollands before returning to his home town where he set up shop in the high street. Most of his early guns were back actions, of course, on the Holland style.'

By now you are at the game-cart and as you slip the offending piece into its cover he presses on. 'I imagine that must date from about the turn of the century?'

'Er, yes more or less, I think.'

'Well, the Damascus barrels suggest the 1800s but then Potter didn't adopt the sidelock action until it was fully perfected because he was elderly by then and sceptical about new developments. While he was a good smith he didn't register many patents in his own right.'

EVERY THING ABOUT SHOOTING

THE HISTORY OF BIG BORES

Bryn ©

48

There is a brief respite while you are ferried to the next drive in separate vehicles but as you both de-bus for the stroll to your next peg, he's back on your elbow. 'His dislike for the modern may stem from his experience with the only significant patent that he did register which was for a pinfire gun in the early 1860s. Pinfires were thought to be going to be the new big thing but the whole enterprise unravelled and Young jolly nearly lost his whole business which would explain why he didn't rush to adopt the new technologies.'

The start of the drive interrupts his flow and while the shooting continues you wonder desperately how to stem the tide.

You might as well try to dam the North Sea. Elevenses brings a new chapter and a new generation. 'Potter was joined in the business in his later years by his elder son, also John. John didn't do his apprenticeship in London, at least, there is no record of him in the registers. It is entirely possible that he might have learned his trade in the Birmingham end of the business, for it is certain that when he eventually took over the business from his father most of the guns sold were made elsewhere and merely stamped with the firm's name before delivery to customers.'

Fascinating. Marvellous. How very interesting. I really must just go and chat to.... But he is not so easily deterred.

'The original pinfire guns, of course, are quite rare now. They are particularly popular among certain sections of the American market. There are some very interesting websites, actually. I could suggest some to you, if you were interested?' Er, well, actually, you know, I just picked it up at an auction as a bit of fun, really. I'm not sure that I want to ...'

But it is already too late. He's scrolling through reams of pages on his mobile phone. By lunchtime he will have chapter and verse not only on your gun and its maker but will have signed you up to the annual news letter of its appreciation society. And by tea he'll have got you a valuation, two insurance quotes and news of a possible pair to it in Timbuktu.

Just focus on the pheasants. There's really nothing else you can do.

THE CRIPPLE STOPPER

He may be your host. He may be your skipper. He may be a relative; by blood or marriage. Or he may even be all three. He may even be a she. And still be all three. Or a spouse. It doesn't matter what he is; or she. What he does though is that he hoves up in your rear view mirror just as you are setting out your stall for one of the signature drives and feeling quietly comfortable about having a bit of serious fun over the next few minutes. You've had a couple of good drives already and your hands are warm and dry; your eye is in and your shoulders are loose. You are in good shape and all is well in the world. And then he slaps you on the shoulder and he says, 'I'm just going to slot in here behind you and cripple stop, since I think you might be a bit busy. You don't mind, do you? Some damn fools do. Just ignore me. I shan't get in your way. I'll just loiter about and help out if necessary. Heads up. Eyes front. Game's afoot, what! Over!'

And so it begins. And already you are in a world of pain. It's no fun having someone on your shoulder at the best of times but when it is your host, skipper, relative by blood or marriage or – God forbid – a spouse, one does tend rather to go to pieces.

It doesn't help, of course, that the cripple stopper is only ever armed with a peashooter. 'Oh, I didn't bother bringing out the big gun today. I'm not really shooting after all. Just tidying up a bit here and there where necessary.

Grabbed one of the boys' guns. Only got a pocketful of shells. Handful really. Just for emergencies.'

Trouble is, you know perfectly well that he's just as deadly with a little gun as he is with his own. Probably more so, if the truth be known, since his own gun is an elderly and weighty 12 gauge side-by-side while he is now waving a perfectly lovely little O/U 20 bore which, if we are honest, we all know is a joy to shoot with even at the veriest rocketer. And that pocketful of shells are not boys' loads after all. They're 30 gm if they are an ounce and the boy in question uses them to knock down pheasants well beyond his neighbour's peg when he's in the line.

So, at this stage, you are uneasy and on edge and less being backed up than cut down. Added to which when you do glance round to see where he has stationed himself he has promptly moved and you only find him again when he shouts 'Over!' at you from somewhere else before clouting a handsome cock right over your head.

'Sorry!' he cries. 'You didn't seem to see it! Weren't you ready? Over!' and another bird bounces behind your peg. Your peg, mark you, yours. Turning back to your front, you attempt to address your birds with a proper determination. But it is already too late and as you tail the next and wing another, he converts them into an elegant right and left.

'Just as well I was here, really. Bad luck! Whoops! Gottim! Come on, old chap, get stuck in.'

Well, you try, don't you? You do the best you can. But under the circumstances, your best isn't your best by any means. Indeed it is scarcely even good enough as the cripple stopper wades in behind you and nails bird after bird, left, right and centre and drops the lot just behind your peg. Your peg. It's not poaching. It's not even gamesmanship. He actually does think he's helping out. But your hands are now cold and damp, your eye is firmly off the ball and your shoulders are getting tenser with every bang and thump just behind you.

And by the time the whistle – or as it might be the horn – goes you have been comprehensively crippled and stopped. That's what he does, the cripple stopper.

THE PARTRIDGE SHOOTER

If your grouse shooter is a steely eyed, whip thin moorland athlete poised in the heather like a coiled spring, your partridge shooter is another matter altogether. Your partridge shooter is dapper. Neat and tidy. Lightly clad; but smart, of course. Flannels rather than tweed, perhaps. Shoes or short boots rather than wellies. Fit, for sure; tensed, certainly; ready, always; but the partridge shooter relies less perhaps on strength and power and more on technique and agility. It's all in the footwork and the quickness. More featherweight than heavyweight. Duck and weave and bang-bang! Twist and turn and bang-bang! Move and shoot. Shoot and move. Bang-bang! here. And bang-bang! there. Here a brace and there a brace.

Big guns are not the answer. These are not stratospheric pheasants needing long barrels and heavy loads. These are partridges bursting over a hedge. What you need is fast guns and light loads. Quick hands and a clear eye. And total confidence. You can't shoot partridges over your head. Nine times out of ten you'll miss in any case because what you are trying to do is catch a golf ball at full tilt with a squash racquet. It can't be done. And if you do actually connect with one it will disintegrate in an embarrassing cloud of feathers because it will be no more than a few yards off.

So partridges have to be shot at forty-five degrees or better. And that means not far above the hedge. The hedge should be high enough to mask you from the partridges and to mask the beaters from you. If you are doing it right then your shot will not be far above the heads of the approaching brushers. But if you are doing it right, then they won't have a moment's concern. And they'd best not have.

Top partridge shooters seem almost not to move. Their gun starts at the high port. When the whistle goes to signal an approaching covey the stock is tucked comfortably under the armpit, left hand extended, weight over the left foot, barrels level with the top of the hedge. When the birds burst into view the stock moves perhaps six inches into the shoulder and the muzzles perhaps half that to cover the leading bird – bang! – and the slightest twitch of the bores towards the second target and – bang! It is possible to spin on one heel while reloading the choke barrel and take another bird quickly behind but the partridge is a noble bird and an honest quarry and does not deserve to be shot in the back. Better therefore to reload and refocus on the front. Peeep! Bang! Bang! Pee-eep! Bang! Bang! Here a brace. There a brace. Bouncing onto the stubbles just a few feet behind the peg.

Which is why the partridge shooter's dogs lie not on his peg but in front of it. Ten or twenty feet away and looking back to where the birds are falling, marking their fall and biding their time before the pick up to come.

The drives are not long either. Everything is brisk on a partridge day. Snappy. There is no loitering over lunch either; and not too heavy on the claret either. You don't want to slow up – or slip up, for that matter. Keep it smart, keep it tight. That's the ticket. That's your partridge shooter.

TEAL APPEAL

He sits in the midst of the reeds on the corner of the pond at the top of Ten Acre. Not for him the blistering gale on the howling saltmarsh. This is duck shooting but it can scarcely be called wildfowling. The birds are wild, sure enough, but this is not the environment where the great bearded men with their big boots and huge guns and salt in their teeth come to fowl. This is a different paddling of fowl altogether. The pond itself is little more than a scrape. Perhaps twenty metres across at its widest point and little more than a foot deep in the middle. Mud permitting, you could walk across it in your wellies with reasonable confidence.

A scoop or two of barley has been cast into the shallows morning and evening since the end of harvest and the teal have been just lapping it up. There have been nights when he has walked up here after dark and when he flicks on the lamp the whole surface of the pond has just peeled away as one to wheel up and round across the moon. And yet he has waited and watched and fed. The banks have been strimmed except for the two or three convenient patches of reed that contain the blinds, each three sides of willow panel with a hook for the cartridge bag and room for the dog at his feet.

The moon is almost full and a decent wind is setting the reeds a'rustle. The sun is still setting amid a blood red western sky and the pheasants are calling to one another as they go up to roost. The duck won't be along for a while yet. Not until the pheasants' last hurrah, when the duck star puts in an appearance. If you haven't seen a duck within twenty minutes of spotting the first star, there won't be one along tonight.

He looks at his watch. The pheasants are calling fit to bust. He checks the loads in his gun and settles the dog, who is fidgeting at the sound of so many pheasants in the vicinity and not being allowed to get involved.

Finally every cock bird on the place lets rip in a final cacophony of ululation. After it subsides the silence is deafening. Almost oppressive. An owl floats by and elicits a salute from the shadow waiting in the reeds. A bat flits overhead and the barrels twitch toward it as the tension mounts. Then 'wiff-wiff-wiff' and there are teal briefly outlined against a passing cloud. He scans the horizon for a glimpse of them again. It's hard to pick them up against the distant woods. 'Wiff-wiff-wiff. Pishsh. Pishsh.' Damn. Damn. Damn. Two on the water already and never caught a sniff. Still, let them be decoys. He can hear them paddling about and preening and guzzling barley. 'Wiff-wiff-wiff-wiff.' Here's another bunch. This time they wheel across the moon and the next thing he knows they are poised almost stationary directly above the hide. The gun goes up and they stand on their tiny tails and climb straight at the stars. The first shot is a snatched response but the second stops a tailender in his tracks to fall with a splash into the water. The dog is ready to go but a restraining hand steadies him. 'Wiff-wiff-wiff-wiff! Pishsh. Pishsh. Wiffwiffwiffwiffwiff!!' Bang! Nothing. That's teal for you. Whip in, whip your hat off, wipe your nose and whip out again.

After half an hour of wiffs, bangs, pishshes, wiffs, bangs and very occasional splashes it is over. The dog finally gets in on the act and a handful of tiny glistening teal go into the game-bag, and man and dog turn toward the distant lights of home.

Beaters' Banter

'I wish I 'ad their lunch,' says the youngster, from his perch on the top of the round bale. 'Beef an' Yorkshires an' all the trimmins. An' wine an' that. An' crumble for afters. Yummee!'

'You get yourself on the outside o' yon sarnie, young George, an' stop climbin' on them bales or yer'll be on yer erse. Your Nan'll have beef pudden fer ye when we get home, never you mind.'

'Will they be long, d'ye think, then,

Grandad?' says George, as he slides down the bale into the middle of the group.

'Oi! You mind ma' bloody tea, young George, or I'll 'ave yer,' growls Big Mick who drives the sugar-beet lifter and beats on shoot days with his trio of smart Springers. 'They'll be back when they've a mind to, I dare say. They'll want to get another couple o' drives in yet an' it'll be dark by half three.'

'They'll need another couple o' drives, I reck'n, if'n they're to get the bag,' says Timbo, who is a mechanic at the garage in the village. 'Wha' are they on for then, Tim?' asks Big Mick. 'I thought I heard Alec say they was after two-fifty. Is that right, Alec?'

One of the keepers looks round from where he is stringing pheasants in the game larder. 'Aye, two-fifty's the target right enough. Martin's doin' 'is nut though as to where 'e'll get 'em. They can't hit a cowshed from the inside, this lot.'

'Ar' thee t'merchant wankers again then? Or is it t'Germans?'

'It's the City crew, Mickey boy. Did you not see the cars in front of the house? Bloody Astons an' Ferraris an' Vogue bloody Range Rovers as far as the eye could bloody see. Blas' there's some money in that bloody lunch room, I'll tell ye.'

'Tha's as mebbee, Alec, but they can't shoot for toffee, can they? That flank Gun at Jubilee? 'E must a' had thirty shots on the corner there, you know where they break back across the new plantation. Never touched a feather. Bang-bang! Bang-bang! Bang-bang! No wonder Martin's doin' 'is nut.'

'We could always put them through the gardens, I suppose, as a last resort,' suggests Grandad. 'Could we not, Alec?'

'We may have to yet. We'll see if a decent gargle at lunch has got 'em in the mood.'

'I'll tell you what put me in the mood. Did you see the fancy piece standin' with the bloke on Three last drive? Bloody Norah! I came out of the brambles on my hands and knees and, I swear, I thought I'd died and gone to heaven.'

'You will die, Timbo, if your missus hears you've 'ad yer stoatin' boots on again, matey.

An' ye won't be goin' to heaven neither.'

'No. 'E'll be in bloody casualty wi' 'is balls in 'is 'and!'

'Eh up, lads. Here comes Martin. Face like thunder. I reckon it'll be a stroll through the gardens for us right enough. Alright, young George? Got your flask and your lunchbox? OK, fetch your stick and we'll be off then.'

THE GAMECART DRIVER

Thank you, sir, thank you. Fair handful you've got there. You must have had a bit of a moment, I dare say? Number eight, you say? Well, there you go. You never can tell, really, can you now? When the lightning's going to strike, eh? You stand on four and five with your heart in your mouth and bugger all happens and then just when you are supposed to be out in the bundoo and beyond, they all come your way. Still, you seem to have made a decent enough fist of it, sir. They can't have been easy as all that, whipping round the corner with this bit of a breeze up their tails.

Mark you, it's been known to happen like that. I well recall when his lordship's father had that new belt planted along the front, like. Old Mr Morton – he was his lordship's head keeper at the time – Morton said it would never work. 'They'll never come over the top o' them new trees,' he said, 'you mark my words, boy, they'll slide out the side like as not.' And his lordship just says 'Well then, if they do, they do and the flank Guns will have a bit of fun when they least expect it, Mr Morton, and what can be wrong with that then?' And old Morton just sniffed and his lordship told them to plant that new belt right across the front anyway.

As it turned out they were both right as it happens. Sometimes they come over the top like his lordship thought they might and sometimes they slide out the side like Morton said they would. Especially if the wind is a bit nor'

east as she is today. Still, that's a bit of luck for you then isn't it, sir? Have they got any more to come then, sir, do you know? The other Guns? All done, you reckon? Very good then, sir.

Yes, it'll be Jubilee next and then I think it's Caesar's before lunch. Moving up two, are you, sir? Well then, if you were number eight here you'll only need a handful, I dare say, for Jubilee but you'd best take the bag for Caesar's. Why Caesar's? 'Cause it backs onto the old Roman road, sir. 'Render unto Caesar!' as his lordship used to say when he shot there. If he had a good stand he'd toss a shilling into the brook at the end of the drive and say 'Render unto Caesar!'

It's a lovely drive, Caesar's. 'Specially at this time of the season. Once the leaf is well off the tree and the birds get up good and early. You can see 'em coming from a fair way off and that flusters some of the Guns. 'Wait till you see the whites of their eyes!' his lordship used to say, and then it was back and forth with the guns till they was almost too hot to manage. No, we didn't shoot double guns all the time by any means. Probably only the big shoots in December, but we very often only shot six Guns in any case. Just his lordship and a few friends really. And some of them could shoot, couldn't they just. I remember one, Colonel Beckett? Bennet? Benson? I forget quite what, he'd lost an arm in the war and shot one handed with a pair of little 16 bores with his driver loading for

him. Damn, he could shoot. Knock 'em down
from all angles, he could, one arm or not. Lovely
to see, it was.

Righty ho, sir. Best be getting on. Remember,
sir, a handful for Jubilee but best take the bag
for Caesar's. See you after, I dare say.

THE TRICK SHOOTER

The trick about the trick shooter – or about the trick shooting – is that really it's not a trick at all. There is no illusion and he hasn't got another one up his sleeve. There isn't any trickery. That's the trick. It's just an astonishing facility backed up by lots and lots of practice. Years and years of practice. Honed and polished by doing these displays up and down the country for more years and years. What it is, is a display of shooting raised to an art form. About as far removed from what the rest of us practise as any trapeze show or jumping a motorcycle over half a dozen buses and a caravan.

If there is anywhere where artifice is involved it is in the banter. The banter is an important part of the display. The occasional, very occasional, missed target is glossed over by a deprecating reference to last night's party or increasing age and infirmity but the chat is really just a ploy to cover the quick reload of the pump action so that the sequence can be undertaken again in double quick time and this time nothing gets away. And all this from the hip, mark you. There isn't any obvious aiming involved but a brisk walking pace with the gun swaying back and forth like a conductor's baton. 'And a one, two, three, four, five, six, seven! And I thank you!' Bish-bosh-bish-bosh-bish-bosh-bish! 'Oops a daisy, that's a runner!' Clunk-click-bosh! 'Got 'im that time!'

The quickness of the hand deceives the eye and the eye can scarcely believe what it is seeing. That's why we journeyman shooters in the audience who reckon that a left and right once in a shooting day is something to remember for the rest of the season want it desperately to be a trick – because otherwise it would beggar belief. It does beggar belief as a matter of fact.

Of course he's been world champion at this discipline and that more times than you can shake a stick at and as we all know world champions are cast in a different mould altogether. They're not, of course, they just take your basic skill and work on it over a period of years, devote time and effort and blood, sweat and possibly tears to it, until they are better than all the rest. It all starts with a talent, for sure, but it is finished with hard graft, ferocious concentration and relentless practice.

The fruit and veg section is a hoot as a variety of produce is chopped to coleslaw at arm's length and head height. The cabbage never fails to impress.

It is also a salutary reminder for those in the audience, especially, though not exclusively, the young, of the awesome destructiveness of a shotgun at close range.

And the finale is as impressive as any fireworks display and the applause is as generous as it is deserved. 'Thank you very much. Enjoy the rest of the fair. See you again at two o'clock.' And tomorrow and the next day. Graft and craft. Can't beat it. Don't miss it. He never does. Astonishing.

PAW BY PAW IN 4×4

'Iwonder how long they'll linger over lunch then?' muses Teal the cocker as he chews at the burrs in the hair about his ankles. His father, Drake, looks at him fondly from the pile of sewelling where he has curled up out of the wind behind the cab and where he can feel the gently ticking warmth of the gearbox easing the chill out of his weary legs.

'Not long, I shouldn't think. It will be dark by half three and they'll want to get another couple of drives in before they finish, unless I'm mistook.'

The black Labrador resting his head on the tailgate yawns wide and long. 'When we wus pickin' up in't Yorksheer they never stopped for t'lunch at all in't December. Shot through and fed 'isselves after, they did.'

'Sure enough, General,' says Drake with a smile and a raised eyebrow, 'and the pheasants in Yorkshire are higher and faster than any-where else and the hills are steeper and the days longer. Like your stories, mate.'

'Naw,' says General, aggrieved 'when Ah wus at Ripon, we never did stop for t'lunch. Tha's so, in't it, Major?' Another Lab looks round from where he is keeping an eye on the young Jack Russell who has been edging towards the cock bird lying beside him.

'Oh aye, Gen lad,' says he, 'proper days them. Never stop for nowt oop thur. Start at nine, three drives, drink and a biscuit, two more drives – an' bigguns an' all, pheasants here,

there and bloody everywhere – soup an' a sausage roll an' two more quick 'uns to finish. Booger me, but we used to pick a rum lot o' birds on them days. Mebbe two or three dozen a drive, if us was behind one o' the busy Guns. OIIIIYYyyy!!' he growls at the terrier who has the cock's tail feather in his teeth by now. 'Yew leave that bloody cock alone, boy, or yew'll have me to answer to. Tha's my bloody boss's bud an' no booger touches it, d'ye hear?'

'I was just going to give it a bit of a lick, honest,' squeaks the Jack Russell as Major fixes him with a beady eye, bares his teeth and rum-bles at him.

'Well, find your own to lick, matey boy, tha' 'un's with me, see?'

'Aye, mate,' says General, 'an' a rum lot o' brambles they'd be fallin' in an' all.'

'Now, don't tell us, the brambles are thicker in Yorkshire and the thorns longer and sharper, right?' pipes up Teal. Drake cuffs him with a broad paw. 'Sure they are, lad, and the grass is greener to boot.'

'Oh, come on, come on,' says Teal, 'I want to get going. Come on, Dad, can't we get going? Pleeeeaaase?'

The curly GWP in the corner suddenly cocks an ear and uncoils herself. 'Echskewse me, bot I sink zat ze gennlemen iss returnink. Ja. Iss so. Perhops to schtand to, ja?'

Teal gives her a long look and makes hump-ing motions. 'I'll stand to for you, Duchess, given five minutes alone. Phwoah! Hey! What about it?'

The GWP simply stares at him and stretches. 'Anytime you vish, Herr Duck, bot iff I see you fost, you vill be – how iss zat? – varing you bolls ass a het? Ach so, hier are kommen ze gennlemen.'

Hello there, you dogs. Have you been behaving? Are you ready? Shall we go and do some more shooting? Shall we? Shall we? Shall we? OK, chaps, load up. Coronation Wood then.

THE KEEPER'S WIFE

Beverly is a country girl born and bred. And yet even her country upbringing didn't altogether prepare her fully for the rigours of a keeper's life. Or, more specifically, a keeper's wife's life. First of all there is the isolation. The cottage is on the back beat of the estate and while it is a picture book bucolic rural idyll with its twisted chimney pluming gentle woodsmoke and its vegetable patch neatly disposed behind with the chicken run and the kennels beyond; it's a long way from anywhere. The most basic journey requires a car and with Brian needing the truck most days the weekly shop has to be planned well in advance and her social life is mostly confined to the dogs. Then again the dogs themselves keep her fairly well occupied. There are the spaniels creating mayhem first thing and the labs to be exercised and she still has to keep an eye on the terriers, who will devote any instant of unsupervised time to chewing whatever they can reach and despite their tiny stature they can reach a good deal.

And there is the rest of the daily routine to be worked through. The woodbaskets have to be kept filled if the hot water is to be hot when necessary and that veggy patch owes its plentiful charm less to luck than to diligent management. And while the toil varies with the seasons, every season brings its own routines and few of them seem to involve nine to five or anything approaching it. Beverly was an energetic and efficient employee at the local seed merchant's before she married but she tidied her desk each evening and she had the weekends to herself.

Now the week runs for a full seven days and by the late spring seems to take up most of the hours of the day into the bargain. There is the unremitting war on vermin. The traplines and the rat poisoning. Hedges may be being grubbed out on some estates but here they are still abundant and each side of each hedge must be baited and trapped in order that the birds have the best possible chance of nesting suc-cessfully. The caught up hen pheasants must be fed and watered and the eggs collected and rinsed and committed to the incubators. The rearing sheds have to be cleansed and disinfec-ted and the stocks of sawdust laid in for the chicks. Then there are the pens to be mended, prepared and cleansed before the young birds arrive in summer and by early autumn they are into feeding and foxing and there is still the need for poacher patrols this close to the town with all the stress and tension that implies. And then the shooting season is upon them once more and the whole shoot moves into over-drive.

Beverly has had to develop a bunch of new skills to match her new life as a keeper's partner. Keeping the dogs up to snuff with regular training is just the start. She pitches in with the bitting and dosing where necessary and she's no slouch with a strimmer or even the chainsaw where needs must. She knows how to handle a lamp. And then there is the constant need to provide sustenance for the inner keeper. Brian likes, indeed needs, his three square a day and being a committed worker himself he has a tendency to get through work clothes at a rate of knots. So there is always a cake on the table and a stew on the stove when he comes in and a fresh shirt for him when he goes out.

It's full time job alright and it is set to get fuller when the gentle swell about her middle materialises with all that implies. The budget will tighten then and the work will increase beyond measure but she looks forward to it with mounting delight and relishes the challenges to come.

That is a keeper's wife for you.

THE RURAL CRAFTSMAN

Derek is rural crafts. In fact, make that RURAL CRAFTS. Writ large. Or perhaps ᚱᚢᚱᚨᛚ ᚲᚱᚨᚠᛏᛊ to be exact since the addition of as many twiddles and curlicues as you can shake a seasoned and well turned carved ram's horned stick at is meat and drink – or rather traditional fayre – to Derek. From his Cornish tin miner's sabots through his stained and worn farrier's apron via the handspun and organically fruit dyed home knitted cardy to the worryingly stained rabbitskin cap by way of eelskin leggings, moleskin breeks and a furze of ginger beard and the inevitable ponytail Derek is everything that the visitors to the Rural Crafts tent at the Country Fayre expect in a fully paid up homespun English rural eccentric.

Today Derek is busying himself building a coracle. He squats in his allotted corner on a rough hewn wooden stool surrounded by woodshavings and with a selection of strange and fearsome looking tools. Here a spooling tether. There a wrenching mattock. Now a trunion saw. In a bucket nearby there floats a mass of what to the untrained eye look not un-like goat scrotums. Quite right! In due season they will be stretched, tensioned, split, twisted, chewed and plaited before being used to down-bind the crossmembers to the subframe before the final caulking of the hullhides with the fretcombs.

This is how Derek responds to the questions that the shuffling crowd occasionally lob at him.

''Ere mate, wossat for den?' as it might be, from the adolescent with the Iron Maiden T shirt and enough ironwork in his features to make a halfway decent garden seat. Derek glares briefly through his bottlebottom specs which have been carefully whipped at the corners with horsehair 'That, sonny, is a leisterer's glaive. It's for spearing salmon by night by the light of a burning torch. Though I dare say it might be handy when the reivers come to call looking for blood and women, come to that.'

'Yer bleedin' whart?' and the kid is gone, to be replaced by a golden headed toddler whose mother exclaims 'Oh, do look, Jocasta. Here's an old man making fairy boats for elves.' Jocasta duly looks and, seeing Derek looking back, promptly bursts into tears. Derek bows once more to his task and assaults the branch he is whittling with a renewed and slightly hostile vigour.

Derek's summer is spent following the rural crafts marquee from show to show, from game fair to country fair to craft fayre. Sometimes he weaves, betimes he coracles. Here he spins and there he turns on the traditional beechwood foot-operated treadle lathe. Now making authentic Norse leatherwear; then creating orig-inal Celtic jewellery. Yesterday a woodsman; today a potter; tomorrow a cobbler. Always, to his lasting disappointment, persistently and irrefutably Derek. Throughout this period he lives in a real Mongolian yurt, cooks old English recipes on an open fire, eats off a wooden plate with iron tools and drinks mead and cider from a horn cup.

Come September Derek returns to real life as deputy head of Design and Technology at a Home Counties comprehensive and an unremarkable semi on the executive estate nearby that is extensively furnished by IKEA (or perhaps that should be IᴋᴇA), which perhaps demonstrates that Derek is closer to an old Anglo-Saxon villager recently invaded by Vikings than even he thinks he is.

THE GROUSE VIRGIN

Don't swing through. That's the sin of all sins. Swinging through. Your neighbour, that is. In the butt on your left and slightly above you; and down there on the right. You can shoot there and there, of course, and there and there. But if you should swing through there or there then you'll never be asked again. It's a mystery why you were asked this time. I mean to say,

he's an awfully nice chap, your host, and positively rolling in it obviously, but why you? He's more acquaintance than friend really, so why?

You might say why worry? You're here after all, and that's the thing. In a grouse butt, on a moor with the early mist still hanging about on the tops. Fore and aft great sweeping rafts of lovely purple heather and any minute there may be, almost certainly will be, grouse. For the very first time. Ever, ever, ever. Just don't swing through, whatever you do. Don't worry. Relax. It's just that everyone else seems so, how shall one put it? – professional. As they sat about in the hotel last night joshing and quaffing. Do you recall old Jacko's right and left at Dallowgill? One in front and one behind and then knocked cold by his first as it hurtled into the butt. Ha! Ha! Ha! And what about Tufty's hatful? Three with one shot, two with the next and both the ones he was aiming at over the horizon and far away. Ho! Ho! Ho! But I bet neither of them ever swung through. 'Lord, grant that I may shoot a grouse, or three perhaps, or even better, drop a handful in the heather. But I'll gladly just have two, if you stop me swinging through.' The grouse shooter's prayer, by yours truly. Just relax. Look at him, down there, sitting on his shooting stick, gun resting on the edge of the butt, calmly smoking and watching the horizon,

gunslip on one side, cartridge bag on t'other. Of course, that's how not to swing through. Set out your stall. Nitwit. Beginner. Eejut. Sleeve there and bag there. That's better. Just a few more shells in the pocket perhaps. Stop fidgeting.

Wowossat? Grouse? A bee, you twit. Calm down or you really will shoot someone. Probably yourself. In the foot. Bang! Bang! Ba-Bang! Bang! What? Where? Who? The other end of the line. Can't see. BANG! BANG! Blimey! That was next door. Damn, was that a grouse? Were those grouse? Are these grouse? That was; those were; these are a cloud of midges. Those on the other hand are grouse. Where…? Which…? What…? Bang! Bang! Oh god, did I swing through? I don't think so. I don't think I did. Are those grou…? Strewth, they really do go, don't they? I mean everyone says they do but until you actually see them. Blimey! OK, sixty yards out. Grouse wear spats. And… Wow! Was that me? Did I get it? I think I did. I did. I got one. I shot a grouse. Damn. Bugger. Spats. Spats. Spats. Hey! I shot another one. Two. Lord, I'll gladly just have two, if you stop me swinging through. That's three. Three then, I'll settle for three. Four, five then. Hey, was that a right and left? I are a grouse shooter. I are a grouse shooter. Five down first drive. OK. Calm down. Just don't swing through.

ALL THE GEAR...

There is no doubt about the equipment. The shiny 4×4 even has mud spatters behind all four wheels; although they were probably sprayed on by a little man in Fulham when it was last serviced. And the tweeds shriek quality – and cost. Beautifully cut in muted Donegal they are a soft testament to the real art of tailoring. And with a matching cap. Which is a clue as to what is to come because, as any commentator will observe, what distinguishes the guests from the estate staff is that only keepers wear livery. With a matching cap.

Long boots. Though it is a warm day in September and we are only going to be strolling the stubbles from drive to drive after partridges, they back up the first impression, which is of a pastime somewhat indulged but little understood.

The guns, when they emerge, are unremarkable. Not extravagant – though by no means modest either. Middle order. Perfectly serviceable. What characterises them however is the cases from which they are put together and the sleeves into which they are slipped. The fumble as barrels are locked into place might be overlooked – over and unders are sometimes tricky to get right, even for the experienced, but the shiny cases, pristine in every respect, imply few journeys even in the boot of such a commodious shooting wagon. There is not a scuff, nor a stain. No evidence of mud or blood. And the same can be said for the sleeves. No shooter, however posh his shooting, has never laid his slip on the grass. And loaders load. They do not stand swathed in bits of kit. And even if a chap has a chap whose only function is to clean and polish shooting gear, that gear develops a certain patina which is quite different from the gloss of the retail emporium cabinet. As it emerges from the boot each element of the stream of equipment tends to reinforce the fact that it is all owned but little used. Monogrammed cartridge bags and magazines are equally free of scars, and the initials are all his own. It's all new. Brand new. Unused. And that's the key. The lack of use.

This is an occasional shooter. He has all the gear, and the burning question is whether he has any idea. A sportsman or merely a shooter? It might go either way. Those who draw pegs on either side of him exchange glances. A raised eyebrow. A pursed lip. And a silent prayer.

And as the first whistle rings out to signal the approaching coveys a young hen pheasant flops forth across the hedge and answers the unspoken question as it is promptly despatched at point blank range in a cloud of feathers.

All the gear... and no idea.

THE BUTCHER

There are no clues. He does not necessarily carry a repeater and he has no distinct accent or origin. He does not wear a badge. But it is obvious as soon as he belts the first bird of the drive, which was scarcely worth a second glance, much less powder and shot, and deposits it in a gory heap just in front of the line. It isn't difficult to see how he does it. What is harder to understand, what is impossible to understand, is why he does it. He is simply incapable of letting a bird by un-shot. It's not even as if he is an especially poor shot, or even a bad shot. He kills at all heights fore and aft, so why does he have to include birds that scarcely make it over the hedge? If he were to announce loudly that leaving poor birds inevitably diluted the quality of the stock as whole, then it might be possible, might just be possible, to look in the other direction as he massacres the poor, unfortunate and inadequate creatures. If he was of modest means and shot but occasionally, it could, perhaps, be explained as over-excitement; but he is rich enough and shoots a lot – though not, it should be noted – by invitation, but on let days where he executes his allotted quota without fear of adverse comment or a single shred of discrimination and no sort of clemency, flat.

The fact of the matter is he likes doing it. Shooting is shooting and letting off is the thing. The bag is key and the bigger the better; and if he has contributed more than his fair share when all is said and done, then more fool the rest for letting him help himself. And help himself he does. Pheasants in October, without tails, height or the experience to do more than stream from the cover at head height; partridges in January as they mingle with the pheasants in modest pairs in the first flush of a courtship ruthlessly terminated; duck off the farm pond at any time and any distance; all are grist to his grim determination to get his money's worth, or more.

It isn't that he is unsafe. No one could take him to task for a dodgy shot or jeopardising a beater or a picker-up. That would be easier by far. And this is part and parcel of the problem. He's paid his money and is entitled to his choice. And if his choice is to obliterate modest pheasants as they glide through the tops of the Christmas trees scarcely 20 feet up, who can tear him off a strip and send him home? These days?

Which is a pity because it may be that there is embedded deep within the butcher some faint residue of, dare one say it, sportsmanship? Which recognises that a pheasant scarcely out of the pen deserves better than to be minced on its maiden journey and tossed onto a heap for someone else to collect after the drive is over. There may be some glimmer of conscience which calls faintly that a mallard on its third circuit round the pond from which it has been unceremoniously catapulted merits no more than a look and certainly less than an ounce of expensive Bismuth. Could that flicker be fanned to a flame by a well deserved and public dressing down that few of us have the courage to deliver? And for that we are as guilty, almost, as he is. For if we will not make the difficult choice, why, after all, should he? Ignorance may not be much of an excuse, but it is better than none; and what excuse do the rest of us have for doing nothing?

Next time you see him, tell him.

THE MAN WHO KNOWS

He's the man who knows. He knows all the best places to stay within a mile of the Game Fair venue. 'Ah naw all the best places to stay within ten minutes of all the sites, ye see. An Ah books 'em three years in advance agin each time Ah leaves.' Which explains why he is on site in time for an early breakfast at the CLA stand. 'Ah can get in early, ye see, because Ah knows the chaps on the stand, an' they gives me a special pass.' Which is why, of course, he can make an early foray down to where the wildlife artists have their stands and smatter them with red dots like an opulent dose of measles. He might even spring for a major bronze if he's got another house to furnish. 'Ah naw what Ah'm lookin' for, of course, 'cause Ah 'ave 'em send me catalogues before Ah cum, so's Ah 'ave a fair idea of what's about before'and. And they know Ah'll always 'ave a few 'cause Ah always do.' And he always does and is therefore a welcome and, indeed, esteemed client in the many places where he bestows his custom. 'Ah won't pay top whack, o'course, but Ah naws what Ah like an' Ah don't mind payin' a fair price forrit, but Ah won't be 'ad, like.' Nor will he. Nor has he. You don't go building up one of the largest construction firms in the country still in private hands if too many people see you coming. And speaking of large construction firms the man himself embodies the phrase. Big and firm and, well, well constructed. Solid. Victorian almost. Big hands just a generation from laying bricks him-

self. Broad shoulders as used to a hod as they are to the finely wrought jacket of lightweight Donegal. Broad girth that betokens a quaffing man used to his three square a day and carrying the signals of his success before him. Squarely set on a proportionate pair of stout brogues. 'Ah built ma firm likes Ah builds my 'ouses. To last. Ah naws what people want. A bit o' substance for their money. I'nt that right, my precious?'

Precious emerges from the broad shadow cast by her husband rather like a dormouse emerging into the sunlight from its nest. Albeit dormice don't tend to carry quite the collection of diamonds that sparkle about precious's person. As diminutive as he is broad, she cuts a slight figure, draped even at this early hour with a collection of carrier bags. 'Blimey, my precious, there you are. Will you look at you already. Shopping for England, eh, sweetheart?' 'Well dear…,' says precious in a tone that belies her small frame and suggests that himself may not, at home, be altogether master of all he surveys, '…these are the shirts you saw…' 'Always best value, you know, at the Fair, eh my precious?' '…and this is the bottle of whisky you got for renewing your subscription…' 'Always get a free gift at the show, you know, don't we my precious? Worth half the bill, eh?' '…these are your trousers…' 'Last twenty years, they will, you know, my sweet. Marvellous value.' '…and this is your new scarf…' 'You can give me that for Christmas, you know, precious.' '…and I'm

now going to the Game Conservancy to make a major donation on your behalf and to get myself a large gin before lunch.' 'Of course, precious, Ah know you are. Ah'll join you shortly, my sweet. Ah've just got to see a chap Ah know about a couple of things.' Course he does. He's the man who knows.

THE CURSE

It's going to be a great drive. You know it's going to be a great drive because it's been a great day already. The weather is perfect. Overcast, to be sure, but dry and with a good breeze. You know this estate and you know this keeper. And he knows his birds and you know that he knows his birds. And this is a prime peg. You drew an outside peg at the start but you didn't mind because the first drive here is always a feeler drive. The keeper just getting the measure of his Guns. Are they any good or do they have to be on the nursery drives all day? But the team shot well enough to pass the early test. The second drive was a notch up and the Guns dealt with those birds with confidence and elegance too. Then there was elevenses because 'The next drive involves a bit of blanking in, gentlemen.' We all know what that means, don't we? The next one will be a big killing drive. And when the wagon rolled to a halt in the lee of the hanging wood, you just knew this was going to be your moment. You've been here before. Never in the middle of the line though. This is one of the 'A' drives. The crème de la crème. A big boys' drive. You unship the gun from its sleeve and settle your cartridge bag within easy reach for more supplies when the birds really start to come. This is going to be a moment, even the moment. You can almost smell it.

And then it comes. He comes. The curse.

'You won't mind if I stand with you, shall you?' It's the sporting agent. Cruising up to schmooze his client. Do you mind? Damn right, you mind. The last thing you want is someone lurking at your shoulder like a bad smell. No, no. Please no. Not me. Not here. Not now. Not this drive. Pleeeaaase. Head says, no way. Heart says, bugger off. Mouth says 'By all means. Make yourself at home.' Perhaps he will stand well back and keep quiet. But no, he plants his shooting stick and settles himself firmly on your good side, just about where you will want to swing high and hard.

Perhaps he will just sit quietly then. 'Lovely morning so far, I think.' Head says, Yes, yes lovely. All's well with the world and I'm about to have the drive of the season. Heart says, please shut up now. But mouth says, 'Certainly. Splendid. Good.' Oh, let him be quiet now. Please.

'Plenty of birds about. I should think you'll have a good drive here.' Yes, I will. If only you will shut up and let me concentrate. Mouth says, 'I hope so.' But already you know that the moment is slipping through your fingers.

'I've got a very good contact in Argentina if you fancied some doves, you know. Oh, look they're moving. Here they come. Heads up!'

And you try. You really try. But it's never going to work. You are cursed.

'Bad luck. Not to worry. Here's another. Coming left. Sorry, never saw that one. Over. Clipped him. Never mind, I'll watch it. Yes, I think it's down. Oh no, it's running. I'll wave to the picker-up. Hello? I say? Oops, sorry, was I in the way? Shall I go the other side, perhaps? Here's another. Over. Bad luck. Do you want more cartridges? I'll get them shall I? Sorry. Over. And again.' And on and on and on. And on. And on.

'Oh dear, is that the whistle? You never really got on terms with those, did you? Do you need a hand picking up all these empties?' Head says, shoot him. Heart says, shoot him now. Mouth says, 'Not really. Thank you. Perhaps next time.' But there isn't a next time, is there? That's the curse for you. And there's no getting away from it.

DRIVEN SHOOTER

Damien is a driven man. And shooting is what drives him. Or so it appears. Damien began life as a dilettante playboy. Well, obviously he didn't, really. He started life as a baby like everyone else but he very quickly became a dilettante playboy. And as a dilettante playboy, supported by a doting father and the sprawling family property empire that seeped from cement factories at home in Holland across apartment blocks in Germany through social housing in Italy to resort hotels the length and breadth of the Mediterranean, Damien embraced shooting in all its forms with both well-manicured hands. He was a regular visitor to all the top London makers and he accumulated an extensive and expensive collection of guns wherewith to do it.

Of course he shot grouse, and partridges and pheasants. Lots and lots of them. And he shot snipe in the Hebrides, woodcock in Ireland and wildfowl on the Wash. Then he went to Argentina and Colombia and shot a lot of doves. Actually, Damien shot really large numbers of doves. In fact, Damien shot truly heroic quantities of doves. And a goodly number of ducks into the bargain. Then he became more adventurous. He shot guinea-fowl and sandgrouse in Africa. He shot geese in Finland and ptarmigan in Norway and capercailzie in Sweden. He shot quail in Georgia and a turkey in Virginia. He shot duck on the Mekong delta. Then he got a rifle.

So Damien stalked red deer on the hill and roe in the lowland woods. He stalked fallow in the UK and shot them driven in Belgium. He shot wild boar here, there and everywhere in Europe, up, down and across.

And then his doting father expired in dubious circumstances in a hotel room in Amsterdam in the company of a lady other than Damien's mother and the said, sprawling property company duly fell into Damien's lap. At which point Damien stopped being a dilettante playboy and demonstrated a hard-nosed commercialism. Within a couple of years the sprawling property company had become a pan-European money printing machine and Damien began to take his shooting more seriously. He got a bunch of new rifles and started globetrotting and trophy dropping big time.

The Big Five in Africa were a given, and he shot more antelope to use as bait than most hunters take in a lifetime. He bagged sundry bears here and there, brown, black and, in due course, white. Moose and stone sheep in the USA, ibex in Siberia and ghooral in India. Basically, Damien shot the lot. And then he went back and shot most of them again in order to set new records for the scale of his shooting. And in the meantime he still finds time to shoot prodigious quantities of pheasants and grouse and partridge in between.

Damien is a driven man. But he'll shoot them going away as well. Ha! Ha! No, really, he's really quite compulsive. But then perhaps we all are. It's just a question of degree.

THE BAD LOADER

He's not necessarily a bad man. He's just a bad loader. You know he's a bad loader from the very first moment when he takes your guns at the start of the day and slings them on his shoulder. Or rather doesn't. He tries to but they slip off into the crook of his elbow and near as a toucher hit the concrete apron of the yard. His suit is a little too new and his boots are a tad too shiny to have seen much work, and it is clear from the off that he has no real experience flat. He's not necessarily a bad person but he's been co-opted in at the last minute because Archie or Ian or, as it might be, Hamish has pulled a muscle, or put his back out, or developed scurvy, or blown up his truck or whatever and can't make it and so a replacement had to be found at the last minute and at this time of year every good loader in the vicinity has got his diary as full as a full thing on a full day.

And so you are stuck with him. More fool you for not bringing Jimmy or Jack from home and springing for the extra room at the hotel and the proper fee; but if you will try to scrimp this is what it gets you. A bad loader.

You know he's a bad loader when he trips on his way to the first butt and your heart lurches as he almost plummets face first into the heather with the sleeves carrying their precious cargo sliding round his neck to break the fall. You know he's a bad loader as he finally slides out the guns and you hear the long metallic whine as the barrels catch on the buckle. Not once; but twice. And if you didn't already know he was a bad loader, you know now when he dumps the empty sleeves on the floor of the butt behind you. Not because they are the finest sheepskin-lined harness leather and things of great price and beauty because they are not – they are modest enough canvas slips, after all – but because shooting grouse with double guns involves a good deal of dancing about in a butt and having sleeves and straps and tangly things all over the place is a trip waiting to happen with a possible disaster lurking in the wings. And so you retrieve them and lay them on the peat wall at either end of the butt and suggest that you will use them as indicators of the limits of your safe swing. 'You what?' he says; and hands you a gun.

'Perhaps you should load it first?' you suggest as your heart sinks lower still. ''Course I should. 'Course I should. Sorry.' And he fumbles with the buckle of the cartridge bag while the muzzles of the second gun under his arm wave back and forth across your knees until he wrestles it open and discharges a dozen or so shells onto the soft floor of the butt. 'Oops!' he says and bending down to reach for them sticks the barrels firmly into the dirt. 'Oops!' He retrieves the cartridges, hands over two for you and loads the second gun. Then he looks down the sharp end and pokes about with his finger. This is where you begin to fear for your life. 'Now we're ready then,' says he. Already your mind, which should be thinking about coveys of fleeting grouse on the wing, is filled with the possible clink and probable clank of fumbled exchanges and the bowel-freezing prospect of the touch of a muzzle on the nape of the neck as he turns to see a bird fall behind betimes.

He's not necessarily a bad man, he's just a bad loader. 'Perhaps you could just stuff for me until we've got started?' you ask desperately as your life flashes before your eyes. 'You what?' says he. Not necessarily a bad man, just a lousy loader.

THE APOPLECTIC OWNER

At the start of the drive the dog is carefully attached to a large corkscrew that is driven into the ground beside his peg. The dog is duly settled and lies down. All is calm. All is quiet. And then the birds begin to move. As the crackle of shots drifts down the line the dog looks up appealingly at his master. Then a handsome cock rattles towards him which he smartly blats on the bonce and which duly bounces on the meadow a few yards behind their peg. The dog sits up and stares intently at the bird as it lies. 'Siddup!' says the owner, as he reaches out to shoot a hen which lands near to the earlier cock bird. The dog begins to whine and to strain at the lead. 'Siddup! Will you sit up! And be quiet,' growls the Gun. He shoots again. Bang! Bang! No result. 'Mnnnewwwweeuuuu!!' 'Will you be quiet! Siddup will you!' The strain on the leash is beginning to tell and the corkscrew is starting to lean. At the same time, that hen is beginning to perk up and look about. The Gun shoots again and a third bird plonks down close to the others. The dog is now actively hauling on the corkscrew. 'NNNNNGGGGGHHHHH!!!' The hen starts to move.

'Will you just siddup! And BE QUIET!!'
The dog looks apologetic and gives a final heave. The corkscrew gives.

And he's off. And the hen's off and the race is on.

'Wait! Wait, will you! Will you wait! WILL you wait! WAIT! WAIT! Dammit! Will you wait. WILL

YOU WAIT! WAIT!!! Okay. Bring it here then. Come on, bring it on. Bring it on. BRING it on, then! BRING IT ON! WILL you bring it. WILL YOU bring it! WILL YOU BRING IT HERE AT ONCE!!! BRING…IT…HERE! WILL…YOU… BRING…IT…HERE!!!!!! Here! Here! Bring it here! There's a good boy, bring it on then. Good boy. Bring her here. HERE!!!!!! HERE!!!! BRING IT HERE!!!!! DAMMIT!!! WILL YOU GET IN HERE!!!!!! No. No. No. NOOO! Leave it be. Leave it BE! Leave IT BE!! LEAVE IT ALONE!!! LEAVE IT!!!!! LEAVE!!!!! Good boy. Good boy. Steady. Steady. Sit. Sit. Sit. SIT! SIT!! SIT, will you!!!! WILL YOU SIT DOWN!!!! Come in here. Come in here! COME IN HERE!!!! COME IN HERE TO ME!!!!!! You bugger, you. You absolute bugger you. Bring that one on then. Bring it on then. BRING IT ON!!!!! WILL YOU BRING IT HERE!!!!!! WELLINGTON!!!!!!' (Why is it that these dogs always have absurd names? Black as my boot. Boot. Wellington boot. Black. Geddit? Wellington boot? Black? Never mind.) 'WELLINGTON WILL YOU BLOODY COME IN HERE TO ME!!!! COMEINHERETOMEWILLYOUWELLINGTON!!!!! Come on, Welly. There's a good boy, Welly. Come on then. Who's a good boy then? WELLINGTONIFYOUDON'TGET- INHERETHEREWILLBETROUBLEYOUBUG- GERIWILLKILLYOUDEADWITHMYBAREHAND SCOMEHERERIGHTNOW!!!

'Will you come here. WILL you come here! WILL YOU come here!!! COME HERE WILL

YOU!!! HERE!!! WELLINGTON!!!!!'

In the distance a horn signals the end of the drive. At which point Wellington looks around and realises that the proper dogs are now scampering about picking up pheasants here and there and that there is little more mileage to be gained from this game, and he finally returns and stands in front of his master and smiles foolishly and irresistibly.

'Wellington, sit!' Wellington sits. 'Wellington, down!' Wellington lies down. 'Good boy, Wellington. Now will you bloody well behave.' What do you think? In a pig's eye, will he.

THE SHOOTING WIDOW

'Caroline. Darling. Hello. How are you? Well, I'm fine. You know… muddling through. Well, I know. Do you think not? Perhaps I don't exactly sound one hundred per cent but to be perfectly honest I'm actually trying to get over the fag end of the most frightful lurgy. Yes, I know. The children all came down with it over half term and then left me with it as a goodbye prezzy when I packed the little brutes back off. Well, I say I; actually I palmed Lizzie off on the Fothergills – you know Rupert and Camilla? – well, their eldest is in Lizzie's year at Wykeham, you know, so they were going anyway – and Charlie I put on a train. I know he's only fourteen, darling, but how else are they going to learn about anything if they don't try? I mean they're not taught these days, are they? No, Eddie's far too young. What sort of mother do you think I am? No, I put him in a cab. Well, I suppose it is rather expensive there and back but there's a nice man in the village who drives Robert to the airport from time to time so it's not as if one is handing him over to a complete stranger, after all.

No, I'm on a train, darling. Yes, on my way to some freezing schloss in Scotland. Again. Well, I imagine it will be freezing. They usually are. Yes, darling, of course he's shooting again. But it's what they do, isn't it? Oh, some corporate jolly, I imagine. Yes, I shall be sitting around listening to them all droning on about sub-prime this and take-overs that and squeezing this and selling those. Well, you know I don't understand a word, do I, any more than you can make head nor tail of half of what Jeremy talks about. Well, of course I'm in first, darling. I'm sick enough as it is and Lord knows what I'd catch if I was crammed in with the cattle class. I doubt if there's even a seat. They seemed to be stacked in three deep as it went past the platform. I shudder even to think what it must be like. No, I couldn't possibly. I mean to say, you might have to sit next to just anybody, mightn't you? And me with half my jewel box in my bag. Oh yes, darling, it's frocks and tiaras for dinner. Ummm, both nights, would you believe? Showy offy or what? Well, it's just more competition for them isn't it, sweetie? 'Look what I bought the missus with mine. Bigger than yours then!' Oh, I know; it's completely ghastly but you have to play the game, I suppose. No, of course he's not here. No, he's driving up in the Range Rover straight from work. Well, there was a suggestion that I should drive it up and he could fly to Edinburgh and meet me; but I told him, I said there was no way I was driving that bloody tank all the way to Scotland when it was his weekend, after all. Well, exactly, I mean I'd be absolutely knackered and I can't work the sat nav thingy for all the tea in China so I'd probably end up in Timbuktu with his precious guns anyway.

'Well, I expect he will be late, Caro, but it's just a question of being organised. 'Prioritise, darling, prioritise.' That's what he always says, and then when I do – with me at the top of the heap, obviously – he goes all humpy. Anyway, I'm not well and you know how he gets when I put a little ding in any of the cars. You remember the Merc? He went on and on and on about it for weeks. Well, exactly. How else is one supposed to park in Chelsea these days? They should make the spaces bigger. Isn't that why we pay council tax? No, I am not going to bloody load for him. I load the dishwasher, don't I? Well, I do on Petra's day off. Sometimes. Ooh, hang on darling, the little man wants my ticket. I'll call you back.

THE WILY COCK

The wily cock is in his element just about now. The season is well over; which is more than can ever have been said for the wily cock, who very soon learned that going over anything meant being enfiladed from all sides. There was a time, to be sure, in his rash and headstrong youth when the wily cock did allow himself to be hoofed out of his snug winter briar patch by the wet nose of a questing spaniel to join his fellow pheasants in a clattering, strident bouquet over the Guns. But the wily cock saw very soon what the consequence of that was. The highest and fastest brought swiftly low. Golden archangels reduced to orange lumps on the grass by the men with guns. The wily cock was having no more of that.

As soon as he heard the first tap-tap-tap of the morning the wily cock was up and off down the hedge as fast as his legs would carry him. When he spotted the stop at the oak at the bottom end, it was into the drain and past him underground. Once round the danger it was back into the hedge and away up the side of Seven Acre before the first shot of the drive had been fired.

Sometimes, of course, they came looking for him there too. But the wily cock always has a Plan B. As soon as the tractor and trailer pulled up at the top of the spinney, he'd be out the side and floating silently away a few feet above the ground back towards his briar patch. 'See tha' ole cock a'slidin owt the side already, boy?

He knows wha's a'comin, don't he?' And they never found him a third time.

If all else failed the wily cock would simply wait until the tap-tap-tapping was as close as he dared and then the wily cock would fly towards the noise, not away from it. It always seemed to the wily cock that facing a few taps was a small thing compared to the bangs and crashes that waited on the other side of the shelter belt. So the wily cock would stutter into the air for only a few seconds to clear the line before settling back into the undergrowth.

Mark you, he'd very nearly got caught doing it in the back end of January when it turned out that the tap-tap-tapping end of things had quite as much bang and crash about it as the other more distant line and he left the last six inches of his tail and the better part of his pride as a testament to the narrowness of his escape. He even overheard someone say 'Tha' bloody ole cock bird ha' dun tha' ev'ry shoot day this season. I'd a thort we'd a'had him today. Well, g'luck to 'im. Canny ole bugger.'

And the wily cock smiled quietly and tucked himself back into the briars.

And now the wily cock is in his element. Crowing lustily to greet the dawn, rounding up his harem of hens and fighting with the other cocks. Few of them have spurs like the wily cock though and the wily cock sees them off into the undergrowth to lick their wounds soon enough while he makes hay – and more – with the hens they leave behind. He's a handsome lover, is the wily cock, though as soon as the capital act is done he's away back into the meadows after his next conquest without so much as a backward glance. He's a cad and a bounder, sure enough, selfish, arrogant and gorgeous all at once and a sneaking, hedge-hopping, ditch-running, self-interested coward to boot.

But he's a survivor for all that and he's learned what the tap-tap-tapping means of a frosty morning and somehow you have to admire him for that. The wily cock.

STOCKING FILLER

'So who are we waiting for then?', asks Harry as we mill about in the yard for the Boxing Day outing. 'Tim and a friend of Julia's who's been staying for the holiday, apparently.' our host replies.

'Chap friend or girl friend?'

'Girl friend, Tim said. He called me a few days ago and asked if she could come along. Tim says she's an old college mate of Jules'. Seems her old man recently did a bunk with his secretary or some such and so the old girl's on her own at the festive tide. Jules asked her over.'

'Decent thing to do. Mid-life crisis, I suppose. Traded in for a younger model. Lot of it about at the moment. Kids?'

'Tim didn't say, actually. But if she's a contemporary of Julia's they're probably grown up. How old are Tim and Jules' boys now?'

'Not teenagers, are they? Didn't we go to Charlie's 21st last summer?'

'True. So I guess if she has any they'll be off somewhere as well. Hence the lonesome ownsome and Jules' and Tim's Wenceslas gesture.'

'Hmmm. Well, we'll jolly her along as best we can. All one can do. Must be hard though. Middle aged woman, on her own, these days. How old is Julia now? Must be rising fifty, I should think?'

'There or thereabouts, I guess. Tim said, actually, that she's a handsome woman.'

'Covers a multitude of sins, old boy. There's handsome and handsome, eh? Why would hubby seek pastures new otherwise? Greener grass, or what?'

'Tim said that the boys were very taken with her actually. Said she was "Well cool" as it happens. Tim said that when they were playing charades the other night she got The Graduate, you know, Mrs Robinson seducing Dustin Hoffman? Seems she simply blew a kiss at young Charlie, wiggled her hips and crooked a finger and that was it. And Charlie blushed so hard they thought he was having a seizure.'

'Is she going to shoot or beat?'

'Shoot. Tim said she would use the boys' Silver Pigeon. Said she's no slouch in the line, as a matter of fact. The bolter used to shoot a good deal, he said. Loads of money, it seems. Big cheese in the City etcetera. She used to tag along. Big days. Might be quite useful. You never know. Is that a car I can hear? At last. About time.'

'What's Tim doing roaring about with the roof down today? I say, do you suppose that's her?'

'Must be, I guess.'

'Wow! That explains Tim's expression. I say.'

'My word. Who in their right mind would leave her?'

'For anything!'

'For five minutes!'

'And rich with it, you say?'

'So Tim said. I say.'

'You don't by any chance have a comb on you, old chap, do you?'

'Too late. They're coming over. Do put your tongue back in, Harry. And remember to breathe. Morning, Tim! Happy Christmas! And this must be.....?'

WHAT CAN YOU DO?

He slips out of the car like an otter sliding off a rock. A greased otter. And he shimmers over and introduces himself to the Guns there assembled. Warmly. With a warm handshake and a deprecating comment. 'Didn't ought to be here today actually but apparently there was a faller at the last, so I got a call at the last minute. What can you do, eh?'

And his suit is a masterpiece of sporting tailoring in subdued tweed. 'Actually, it's a mohair mix. Weirdest thing. Tailor chappie calls me up and says that some fellow had ordered the fabric and then never turned up for the fitting. He was a bit stuck and would I take it off his hands at cost? Well, what can you do?'

His boots are lined with sheepskin and heated. Heated, for heaven's sake. 'Bit of a prototype. Bonkers idea, I thought. But they insisted I try a pair. They have a battery just in here, you see. Actually they're fantastic, you know. Far too expensive to put into production, of course, but what can you do?'

And the guns, my dears, the guns. The sweetest pair of old English over and unders you ever saw. Balanced like a conductor's baton and glowing like conkers in their velvet bed. 'Well, you know how it is, don't you? My godfather gave me the No.1 as a 21st present – oh, thirty years ago, I guess – and then my gunsmith, who services it from time to time, calls me and says that a chap has walked in with the No.2 and does he think he could sell it for him?

Well, what are you going to do? I mean you have to re-unite them don't you? Really?' Of course you do.

Everything has a story. But the story is much the same with everything. Serendipity looms large in this chap's life, it seems. The Range Rover is a limited edition turbo charged V8 with overdrive. He went down to the dealership to get something quite different, of course, something more modest, actually, he doesn't really approve of flash motors as a rule, obviously, but there was this truck which had just been slashed off the local constabulary's budget. 'Can't have traffic plods cruising about in a drug dealer's car these days can you? Delivery mileage only and going at trade price plus the cost of a respray. Well, I said, what can you do?' His business life – which you piece together, drop by drop, as you are wafted about the shoot in sumptuous leather clad comfort – seems to be the same story of wholly unanticipated good fortune. 'So they ask me to join the board – can't think why, hadn't the first idea about the business, still it was sweet of them to ask – and then I bump into this chap – out shooting actually – and it turns out he's itching to buy the whole shebang. Tons of money. So I passed the suggestion on to the rest of the directors and they said, well, what can we do? Always seems to happen. Every time I get a proper job some bugger turns up and buys the firm. Still, what can you do? Drives my missus mad.'

The 'missus', needless to say, when she arrives to join the fun at lunch, is a drop dead looker who just happens to own a large slab of acres up the road. "Course, she didn't have it when we met at college. Then some cousin or other went a bit off the rails and her aunt decides to leave her the estate. We wondered whether to move up here, actually, I mean, it's a bit of a responsibility what with the farms and the cottages and the shoot and the fishing and what-have-you and the house is a complete millstone obviously, but what can you do? It does come with it's own pub, mark you, so at least I can run a decent tab at my local.' A beautiful girl in possession of a large estate and her own pub then. Well, what can you do?

And guess what number he draws? You guessed it. What can you do?

91

THE PERCY SANDWICH

It is supposed to have started with the Percy brothers – the present Duke of Northumberland, Ralph and his little brother, James – but having, as I do, a real and detailed understanding of the laws of libel and defamation I could not possibly comment on the accuracy of that proposed origination. Though it is accuracy which is the key to the Percy Sandwich and the Alnwick fraternity are in that respect, if in no other, notorious. And in their younger days, so the story goes – or perhaps myth or legend would be the better term, when finding themselves drawn on either side of some more ordinary Shot, they would – no doubt from the very best of intentions and motives and in the best traditions of banter and badinage in the shooting field and in the most gentlemanly way – shoot every bird that headed in any sense toward the unfortunate visitor so far ahead of him that he never got his gun to the present, let alone to the shoulder or beyond.

Anyway, I don't believe a word of it. Obviously. So why the Percy Sandwich should have passed into the language remains, for the time being, a mystery.

What is more certain though is that as a jape among friends it remains right up there with the confetti filled cartridge.

All that is required is that two chaps of undoubted skill and consistent accuracy should, upon finding themselves drawn on either side of a third friend should make the determined decision that said third friend shall not – for the duration of the following drive – be allowed to get a meaningful shot off at an approaching bird. It must be said that the whole thing only really works on very tall pheasants, in open sky, which are flushing only in singletons and pairs and which are making stately progress – rather obviously – towards an individual, the individual, Gun. These sort of pheasants being pretty much the norm in Northumberland hints perhaps at the totally unjustified association with the Percy boys. At which point the conspiratorial neighbours drop them at his feet one after the other.

The point is that the victim – if he has anything about him – will try to up his game and take his birds earlier on and further out. Only to find that they are still dead before he gets to them. And they must be dead. The joke only works if every single bird is stone dead before the sandwich filling has even raised his piece. Let a single one through and the whole thing falls apart. Unless, that is, he then misses it with both barrels – probably from surprise – only to have it rolled up, neat as you like, just behind him after the event.

You can do it if you are double banked too. Except that it doesn't count if the victim is in the second row. That's too easy by half. If he's in the front row though – and the pranksters are behind him – then the effect of the joke is doubled.

Oh, and when I say two chaps of skill and accuracy, I means by chaps, chaps, of course, of either gender. If two lady Guns were to slam the door in such a way on another chap in their middle that would redouble the effectiveness of the jape for sure. And it couldn't possibly be a Percy Sandwich so we'd have to think of a new name for it. Which would be a lot of fun too. Go, girls, go!

THE HANGOVER

Ooooh Gawd! Woddid I do? An' why? Why? Urrgghh! Blurry hell! Ghazzly mizztake. Grape an' grain. Getcha evr'y time. Blurry malt. Damn claret. Blasted Cockburn's blurry vintage. Branny, for Chrizzakes. VSOP. Vicious. Savage. Odious. Poison. Oh, my head. My guts. Mouth like the bottom of a budgie cage. Blurry Cohiba blurry coronas. Should know bedder ad my age. Hic! Oooogh! 'Kin 'ell! Tha's payback. Taste the whole lot over again. All together now.

We've all been there. I suspect. Not yesterday, perhaps. But sometime. The morning after the night before.

The trouble is that when we arrive on the evening before the shoot we are already excited. We are expansive. We are open to suggestion. And our hosts are so generous. Sooo generous. 'Long drive? Must have been ghastly. Have a dram. Calm you down, old chap. Get the brake lights out of your eyes.' And the old boy sloshes Aberlour – or as it might be Talisker or Macallan – into a tumbler the size of a bucket and sticks it into your mitt with a pat on the shoulder and leads you to a chair by the fire. 'We'll just have a spot of supper and early bed. Need to be on top form tomorrow. Keeper is promising great things and even the weather seems to be playing ball.' And he gives the glass a bit of a tap and returns to decanting the Crozes Hermitage. And what with the little smoked salmon canapes and the smoked almonds and the fire the malt slips down a treat and is promptly replenished

with another half pint of the good stuff. Supper – supper, they said – is a sequence of gastronomic delights. A little something with goat's cheese and dressing and a splash – or two – of the Montrachet. Then the partridge with all the trimmings and that Hermitage in a glass the size of a hot air balloon - 'You're looking a little dry down there, old boy. Darling, shove the decanter at him,will you?' Pudding light as a feather; but rich, rich, rich. With cream and a chilly Sauternes. Then the Stilton in all its glory and that damn port and by now you're flying. The anecdotes come thick and fast and everyone is laughing, roaring, hooting till their eyes run. And the decanter goes round. And round. And round. And round.

And then we withdraw back to the fire. And out comes the brandy. You pause. You cavil. You defer. 'But it's the old one, old chap. Last of grandpa's finest. Try a little, why don't you? I promise it won't disappoint.' And nor it does. Or the next one. Or the one after that. Lord Ripon used to retire at 9.00pm and practise changing his guns after a light supper and a glass of dry sherry and Lord Ripon knew a thing or two about this game. We, apparently, know bugger all.

Which is why we are now standing at a peg in a field feeling like death warmed up, with a mounting Vesuvius rumbling in our guts, swigging Irn-Bru and dreading the moment when form, civility and simple good manners will require us to let off the damn gun regardless of the consequences. Which might be severe and horribly public.

The only hope is to make it through to elevenses and hope that a mug of Bullshot, a slug of sloe gin and a sausage will repair enough of the damage to save the morning from being a dead loss and fortify the system sufficiently to be able to face lunch. Oh God, lunch. Oh no. Not lunch. Don't think about it. UURRGGHH! And then, on the chill fresh breeze comes the distant cry, 'OVVERRR!!'

BETTER SAFE...

He stands with the gun tucked under his arm and broken so everyone can see that he is being safe. His eyes scan the horizon but he is not looking for targets but hazards. He sees not pheasants but beaters. He turns to seek out the pickers-up behind him. They may be a goodly few hundred yards back from the line of Guns but you can never be too careful, can you? He checks his neighbours, right and left. And their neighbours. And their partners, spouses, friends and significant others. And their dogs.

A distant whistle indicates the impending arrival of birds, as it might be a covey of partridges or a bouquet of pheasants. He closes his gun – butt to barrels, obviously – and assumes the present position, barrels well up above the tree line. He watches as the birds hurtle past. His neighbours each take a bird but he remains resolutely still waiting for a chance that is safely and properly high enough. Which is really not going to happen very often with a partridge unless you are really lucky with the topography. He might pop one over a shelter belt but he's never going to get seriously involved over hedges. And he'd starve in a driven grouse butt, for sure.

Surely a pheasant will be manageable?

You'd be surprised. This one is too low and is quite properly ignored, he says. That one should be his neighbour's, for sure. That long crosser will be a better bird for the flank Gun. Safety is central to his being but politeness at all times comes a close second. Shooting at your fellow Guns or the beaters or pickers-up may be the ultimate sin but potting your neighbours' birds or what might be your neighbours' birds or which might be perceived as being your neighbours' birds even if the neighbour in question is calling that he is unloaded and needs help, would be almost as unforgivable. In his view.

And it would be hard to disagree with the principle. Of course. But we must not forget that the object of the exercise is to shoot pheasants – or as it might be partridge or duck or whatever and that to ignore those presented to you is also a discourtesy to the keeper and his beaters.

And yet he waits and waits. And waits. And waits. Ignoring this one. Eschewing that one.

Disregarding the other. Neglecting these. Forgoing those.

His neighbours do their best to fill the gap in the line but they are conscious that if he is of the view that his shot would be risky then they can scarcely shoot across him without attracting the raised eyebrow and the pursed lip come elevenses which makes for awkwardness at lunch.

And then there comes a corker. High, wide and handsome. Tall as you like. In fact, it might very well be the bird of the day, could he bring himself to down it.

It is a fabulous pheasant. A huge pheasant. A magnificent pheasant. All eyes are on him. Guns, beaters, pickers-up, partners, spouses, friends and significant others. And their dogs. Fingers are crossed and small prayers offered. Come on. Come on. Come on. The gun comes up. There is a swing. But........no shot. A sigh echoes down the line.

'A little far, I think,' he says, 'one doesn't want to wound, does one? Better safe......'

METHUSELAH

There was a time – oh, many, many years ago now – when Jack used to ride in the wagon with the other beaters; but times change and we have to change with them. Jack hasn't changed one jot, tittle or iota. He graduated, morphed would be the modern term, from beater to picker-up when he got Tern and that must have been three decades gone. Tern was a great dog, the best, and that was the point at which Jack climbed off the wagon and into his battered old van and trundled off to position himself well back behind the Guns where he can watch for pricked birds gliding down beyond the sight of the rest of the field. The van goes everywhere. Not at any great pace, it must be said, but it will go, does go, where shiny four-wheel drives would fear to tread. Tern is long gone now but Jack still has his descendants, Knot, Dunlin and Petrel. They're working cockers. Small, compact, eager, busy. Knot is old now but what he lacks in pace these days he more than makes up for in wisdom. Knot's nose works steadily back and forth under the brambles and when the moment comes his bulk is more than a match even for an energetic cock bird.

Dunlin – Jack's cottage is on the edge of the estuary, in case you were wondering – is in his prime. Fit and agile, he can fetch back a runner from the other side of a field of plough without pausing for breath or carry a duck across a surging tide with equal facility. And still want for nothing more than the chance to do it again. And again. And again.

Petrel is the youngest. She's coming on a treat though and if she develops as Jack thinks she might she may even challenge the supremacy of Tern of sacred memory. There are other reasons too why Jack doesn't ride in the wagon. For one thing the latest generation wagon has a large 'No Smoking' sign in it, being as it is officially designated these days as a workplace, and since a reeking briar is a permanent fixture protruding from Jack's stubbly chin and since no one would have the temerity to suggest that Jack might like to knock his dottle of Irish Twist over the tailgate, and Jack doesn't hold wi' them 'bloody Elves 'n' Safety boogers' anyhow and especially since the van contains all of Jack's things. His stick and his bag and his game carriers and a lot of baler twine for pairing up the birds, and leads for the dogs (not that they need them since they never leave his heels) and his leggings and a spare coat and scarf but not hat. Jack's hat is almost as much of an institution as the man himself. Once it was a trilby; or so it is said. The nap now is so worn and greasy that the original pattern is all but gone. Woodcock pin feathers adorn the band and startling blue jay quills flash among the murk. It's largely held together by Campaign for Shooting badges.

Jack catches up with the game cart at lunch and at the end of the day. On each occasion he

will pull five or six brace of birds from the
back of the van and pop them on board.
Then he will pluck the pipe from between
blackened stumps, push back his hat with the
stem, knuckle his stubble, spit and deliver himself of his opinion of the day's Guns. 'Righ' load
o' jessies, if you as' me. I mus' ha' picked eight
from be'ind Jubilee Strip and no bugger even
come lookin'. They don' gi' a toss, dithee?
An' they can' shoot for toffee. Well, I'll be
ge'in on then.' And he clambers back
into the van and chugs off in a
cloud of diesel and shag.
He must be eighty plus,
nearly ninety. No one
knows, least of all
Jack, and he wouldn't
care less.

The Mainstay

Mrs Stradling is firm but fair. 'Alright everyone, walking at heel then. One, two, three, four, five. Keep those leads short. Martin, try to keep Cassie behind the knee, not bounding about like that. Six, seven, eight, nine, ten. And pause. And SII-IT! No, just a firm push on the bottom, Jemma, you don't have to jump on the poor boy. You're trying to get him to sit, not drive him into the ground like a fence post. Good. Good. Well done.'

Mrs Stradling runs the Brigham and District Retriever Club and has done for two decades. Her own dogs are, naturally, exemplary and she picks up four or five days a week in season on her own estate and other local shoots, and during the spring and summer she runs weekly training classes for working dog owners in the vicinity. She also manages working tests for the club, doing not only the administration but also serving as a judge. Mrs Stradling lives for working dogs.

She has, perhaps, rather less time for working dog owners. 'There are very few poor dogs,' she avers, 'but there are, I'm afraid, any number of poor owners.' Not that there are many poor owners at the Brigham and District Retriever Club. Mrs Stradling's early classes are focused almost negligibly on the dogs but are designed to whip the owners into shape. The pupils may think that they are taking their assortment of mutts, pets, pooches and possibles to classes but in fact the reverse is true. The dogs are taking them to be trained.

All are welcome and as a consequence there is a broad cross-section of the working dog world in terms of both owners and dogs. There is a preponderance of black Labradors, of course, but there are also springers and cockers as well as a brace of golden retrievers, a flatcoat and an Irish setter called Fergus who exhibits all the scattiness that outsiders associate with the breed.

And the owners are a motley crew also. Some are local men and women who work in the vicinity. Derek's a plumber who runs his own business and shoots a bit with a local farm syndicate and beats a good deal as well. He wants his spaniel to pick up for him and join him in the line. Val and her husband run the pub. He shoots and she wants to join him in the field, but with a greater sense of purpose than just as a spectator so her Lab Tara is a key part of the plan. Jemma is only twelve but she and Felix the working cocker are inseparable and are shaping up to be a formidable team. Then there are the non-locals. The area is a popular dormitory for professional types and downsizers and a working dog is a prerequisite for a shift to the country. Hence a bunch of black Labradors. Still, you never know where your diamonds are to be found so all are welcome at the BDRC and in the paddock below the Hall where Mrs Stradling runs her classes and keeps her eyes peeled for potential FTChs to develop and co-opt in due time into the BDRC competitive line-up.

In the meantime, it's back to basics. 'So, walk away from your dogs. Hand up. Keep reinforcing the command. Wait. Wait. Wait. Don't raise the voice, Tim. We're not intimidating, are we? It's a partnership, isn't it, after all, that we want to achieve? Don't chide him. Just take him back and settle him again. And… wait. Wait. Wait. Good. And call them in. Well done everyone. Loads of praise. OK everyone, that'll do for this evening. Same time next week then.'

THE WALKING GUN

'Now for this drive we'll need a walking Gun. Who's No.1? Alex, is that you? I know it's after lunch but do try to keep up. If you go with the beaters, I'll stick the others on their pegs and then nip back round the wood behind you so that I can pick up anything which comes your way. Assuming you hit anything that is, eh? Okay? Off we go then.'

So you go with the beaters and there is a deal of joshing from those you know from other visits here. 'How's the treacle pud sitting then, Alex? That's claggy old plough down the edge of Long Strip. Har-har!' 'Got a few squibs in yer pocket then, Alex? There's a fair few birds tend to cut back across the dog-leg, y'know. Might be a busy old amble, if yer luck's in.'

And so you shovel a few more shells into your pocket and check your belt as the boys line out and start tapping. Then the keeper calls for the start. 'Okay, lads, take it steady and keep the left flank forward. There's a few birds should be in 'ere, so take it easy and keep the dogs close please for the time being. Off we go then.'

So off we go.

And there are a few birds in here and it is not long before they begin to move. They mostly go forward; which is no surprise since that is where they are intended to go and the keeper is an expert in getting birds where he wants them. He'd have them through the Hall window if the boss asked him to.

But they do not all go forward. 'Coming right! Coming right!' A wily cock breaks through the canopy and swings back high above your head. The gun comes up instinctively and he crashes into the plough a good way out and lies still. A glance back confirms that your host is just emerging from the corner of the strip and he waves as his dog begins to charge towards the fallen bird. 'Coming right! Coming right! And again! Right! Right!'

Bang! Bang! 'Nicely done, sir. Thank you." Praise from the keeper, eh. That's praise indeed.

'And again, sir! Right! Right!' And that's another.

And so it goes. The birds keep coming in ones and twos and for reasons that can never be adequately explained you just can't miss them. And even when you do the second barrel folds them up in any event. The host's dog is kept busy gathering them in and by the time you have nailed half a dozen – as well as a couple of very snappy right and lefts – the host's hands are full in every sense of the word. Carrying ten pheasants is never easy, but carting them across heavy plough - after lunch too – is proper work and it is discernibly the case that he is falling further and further behind the line.

'Coming right! Right! And again!' Bang! Bang! 'Well done there, sir. You're on fire this afternoon, like. The boss must have had the good stuff on the table at lunch today, eh? Ho-ho!'

Whatever it is, it's still working. 'Coming right! Giddup bird, giddup! And again. Thank you , sir. Hardly worth me calling them for you, is it, sir? Here's another then! Lovely!'

In the distance, the host is leaning on his stick and mopping at his brow as the dog brings yet another bird to hand and there are another handful already lying dotted about the plough.

'Right! Right! And again! And again! Last chance, sir. Be quick, sir, be quick.'

Bang! Bang! Fast reload into the choke barrel and............Bang! A cheer erupts from the beating line. Moments don't come much better than this. Savour it. Out on the plough, your host's dog is having the time of his life. Your host is having what can only be hoped is a small heart attack.

THE THREADBARE HOST

He is charming and diffident. 'Good morning all. Good morning. Oh, I dunno, we might stumble across one or two, I suppose. Best put the spare bag in the wagon just in case. Keeper'll do his best anyhow.' And you know that it will be a lovely day and you know that there will be birds in abundance because you know that for all the diffidence and charm you don't get a place like this on diffidence and charm alone and that there must be steel in there somewhere behind the charm and diffidence and you know that a chap who has his gravel freshly raked every morning is not the sort of chap who stumbles across anything very much unless he has had it arranged to be there for the particular purposes of being stumbled across.

Why then does he dress as if he has just ransacked Help the Aged in the high street? Actually, why does he look as if he got to Help the Aged in the high street shortly after it had been ransacked and all the really good stuff filched by vagabonds, vagrants and scarecrows? In fact, why does he look as if he arrived after what was left was binned by the management as being beyond the pale of the human wardrobe? Why does he appear to have raided the skip outside Help the Aged in the high street?

The cap has a split up the back because it is too small. Probably made so by the fearsome ridge of darn across the top. The collar of his Tattershall shirt is more tatter than hall and is held together in the absence of buttons by a Hermes tie so thumbed about the knot as to render the original pattern indistinct. The paper-clip cufflinks would be ironic in gold. In grey they are just paper-clips.

The suit, my dears, the suit. It was clearly a thing of beauty once. The Donegal is soft and muted and the cut is exquisite even if it is the thick end of fifty years old. The point is though that there is almost as much patch as suit. The question that floats about is why you would, over time, insert enough patches into an old suit to make a new suit and still not come up with a new suit? How does he do that?

His stockings are a palette of coloured wools whipped into scars the size and texture of hairy caterpillars up and down his shins and his brogues may shine like conkers but they are conkers with more creases and cracks than an elephant's arse.

The estate is pristine. The birds are spectacular. The sport is compelling. The gun room is a testament to opulent but discreet good taste. Lunch is served by liveried staff. The claret is to die for, the port is vintage and the cigars genuine Cubans.

So why the thousand-year-old suit?

THE HOSTESS WITH THE MOSTEST

It is said that men make love with their eyes and that women make love with their ears. And it is never more obvious than when the guest Guns troop into the converted piggeries for their morning coffee and are confronted by Valerie. Mainly they trip on the step. Then they goggle. Then they gibber. Then they blush and hurrumph. And then they goggle some more. And return to gibbering. For whatever it is that makes a chap sit up and take notice – and then trip, goggle, gibber, blush, goggle and gibber – Valerie has it in spades. Doubled and redoubled. And then with an extra helping on top.

It isn't obvious. Val is not, after all, a super-model. Never was. But there is something about her which just makes a chap sit up like a Labrador that has just heard the rattle of the treat jar. Eyes wide, tongue lolling and looking a bit simple.

She's pretty, no error. No question about that. Always has been. Just check out the photos on the sideboard if you ever get into the house proper. Val would have always caught the eye. Slim and fair. And still slim and fair now, a quarter century later. But that is not what stops a chap dead in his tracks. There is a sort of energy about her. A vigour. A sparkle. That makes men want to just scoop her into the passenger seat of a sports car and go VRRROOOOMMMMM!!!! Grace Kelly had it. Natalie Wood had it. Audrey Hepburn virtually patented it. And Val has it. And men quail before it.

And as a consequence the simplest conversation becomes fraught with difficulty. 'Would you like it with or without? Your coffee?' she says. 'Errgh! Umm! Pwoarghhh!' 'Cream? Sugar? How about a bacon butty?' 'Urggh! Yes please. Yum-yum. Gosh! Wow! Ah! Hurrumph!' 'Tomato sauce is on the table. Help yourself to a squeeze if you'd like.' 'Arghh! Hurrumph! Squeeze! Squeeze! Mmmmm! Arrgghh!'

It doesn't help, of course, that Valerie is wearing a cashmere pully and buckskin jeans. They are just what she always wears for a shoot day; being warm and practical and comfortable. And yet they cling like a second skin – as only cashmere and buckskin can – and they reduce every man in the room to a state of Neanderthal fundamentalism able only to see her as a female of the species barely clad in fur and leather, and obviously pining only for a chap with a cave and a club.

You may well ask how she ever ended up with Martin. Martin is a perfectly nice chap. Always has been. But he was never going to set the world on fire, was he? Drifted through school, ambled through college and assumed the mantle of squirearchy without a murmur when he inherited the estate in due course. And yet somewhere along the way he collected Valerie, whom everyone else recognises as being a fizzer of epic proportions, and whom Martin seems scarcely to recognise other than being a jolly good old thing. It defies belief.

Elevenses is a repeat of breakfast. Valerie swings down from the cab of the farm pick-up with soup and sausages and all the Guns go weak at the knees. When she asks Charles if she can hold his sausage while he manages the sloe gin the poor old boy swallows a mouthful of soup the wrong way and near as a toucher expires on the spot.

And lunch is a repeat of elevenses. This time it is Andrew who explodes a mouthful of Stilton across the tablecloth as Valerie leans over his shoulder with a bottle in each hand and asks him if he'd like something sticky to go with his cheese.

Valerie herself seems oblivious to the effect that she has on men; perhaps she assumes that, like Martin, they are oblivious to it too. Or perhaps she believes that all men are just incoherent half-wits who variously trip, goggle and gibber as a matter of course.

She wouldn't be far wrong.

THE LANDLORD

Big Sid is the landlord of the Bull. Big Sid is his name and the Bull is his pub but his name might as well be John Bull for that is who, or what, he resembles, embodies and personifies. His face is red, his whiskers are abundant, his girth is prodigious, his laughter is deep and unbridled and his conversation is as honest as his opinions are unrefined. And his hospitality is legendary in these parts. And he knows what a shooting lunch is all about.

From the moment you enter you know you are in good hands. 'Welcome, lads, welcome!' he booms, beaming, from behind the bar in the snug as the team, Guns and beaters, troops in. 'Lean your guns up against the wall in yon corner where I can keep an eye on them for you while you sup. There's water in the back for the dogs as long as they're all happy wi' one another and I've put the racks out in the scullery an' all if you want to hang up your wet coats for a bit of a warm. Ye can wash up in there as well and what will you be wanting when you come back? Bitters all round for a start, is it? And a Guinness for you, as usual, Pat? Grand. Grand. Grub's just about ready, so you can sit down once you've wet your whistles, boys. Good day, was it? Few birds about, were there? That's grand then. Bit of fun, eh? That's the ticket. There you go, Michael. One away to you. Get your arse in front of the fire but mind you don't peel the wallpaper as you steam! Ho! Ho! Rather you than me this morning, son, eh?'

And he moves around the throng with surprising grace for such a big man, with a tray of tankards on his meaty palm and with his waistcoat straining at its brass buttons while the heavy gold Albert of his watch chain twinkles in the firelight of the cheering blaze in the ingle.

'If you want to make your way through when you're ready, gents. Beef's on the sideboard and there's veg on the table. Maggie will be there shortly with the Yorkshire pud and gravy. There's meat carved but help yourselves. There's plenty, I reckon, so don't hold back. The claret's in the jugs. I opened 'er at breakfast so she should be ready and willing by now, eh? Ho! Ho! Another stout for yourself is it, Paddy boy? Don't hold with the poncey French drink, eh? Ho! Ho! Here's horseradish. Grated it myself this morning. Can't let the girls do it these days or the bloody elves an' safety'll 'ave me licence I shouldn't wonder. I'll just go an' check on the custard, boys. Tuck in, tuck in. Help yourselves to another slice if you feel the need but leave some room for the steam puddings. Treacle sponge and spotted dick. And I've a lovely bit of Stilton for you after. For the real men, like. Ho! Ho! Call that a helping, young Simon? I'd ha' thought your ma would have brought you up better than to insult a man by peckin' at his fare like that, eh? Ho! Ho!'

And the sideboard groans under dark, rich ribs of bloody beef. The 'tates are roasted golden and the Yorkshires are light and brittle. The claret is ruby and warm and the puddings a testament to the nurseries of old England. As the temperature in the room rises, the conversation becomes more animated and when the level in the jugs sinks as the darkness gathers outside the company call on Big Sid to fetch his accordion and give them a tune. And so the evening starts.

For sure, Big Sid charges for his food and drink; but the prices are fair and the portions as generous and ample as the man himself because Big Sid knows that a country pub needs sportsmen just as sportsmen need a decent local. So the good cheer cuts both ways and a good thing lasts for a while longer. Ho! Ho!

THE FORGETFUL GUN

He's late because he forgot to set the alarm clock for the right time and because he left the directions on the hall table in his consequent rush to leave. Which also explains the fact that he is wearing odd stockings and has neither gloves, ear-defenders nor a hat. He has also succeeded in putting his daughter's wellies in the car instead of his own, which given that she is in her teens and a slight girl whereas he used to be a useful enough prop forward to have had a try out with the Harlequins means that he will have to spend the day plodding about in his moccasins unless someone helps him out in the footwear department.

He does have a gun, which is a bit of a bonus but only in the limited sense of its not having a fore-end because he keeps that in a separate safe for the greater security which is fine from the security point of view – not least in terms of the pheasants' resulting continued well-being – but frustrating for him. Not that having the fore-end would actually permit him to shoot at the pheasants because he has packed the wrong cartridge bag and has therefore no bullets to shoot with even if the gun was complete.

Fortunately the rest of us have got used, over the years, to his little foibles in particular and indeed to his utter uselessness in this regard in general. Since almost everyone has brought a spare something in the anticipation – indeed expectation – that he would arrive without something, if not everything, it is simple enough to equip him with the wherewithal to allow the day to commence.

We also remind him that it is his wedding anniversary this weekend. This he stoutly denies until it is pointed out that this particular shoot has been undertaken on the same weekend for more than a decade now, longer for some of the team, and it has always been his wedding anniversary in previous years, so why should it not be the case this season? In fact some of us actually went to his wedding, which he had the poor taste to allow himself to be cajoled into agreeing to plonk into the busiest part of the shooting season and, as a matter of fact, on this very weekend, to the considerable detriment of those of us invited because we were obliged to miss what we all knew would be a cracking day's shooting.

As is traditional he apologises and points out that it was scarcely his fault and anyway he forgot. We tell him to forget it and point out that there are various bouquets and sundry boxes of truffles and a variety of aromatic perfumes lurking among the vehicles which should get him off the hook in this regard when he gets home.

He may be the bee's knees in the boardroom and one of the keenest legal brains in the business Monday to Friday but he's a walking disaster area everywhere else.

Halfway through the last drive he remembers

he's supposed to be at his other child's carol concert at the other end of the country at seven and departs at the gallop in a cloud of dust. He has taken the bouquets and the truffles and the aromatic perfumes, which is just as well because he has left behind his phone, his house keys and his daughter's wellington boots. Just as well he hasn't got a dog.

THE CHARITY SHOT

Ok, there are charity shoots and there are charity shoots. At charity shoots everybody has a go and it's a bit of a laugh and the first prize is a rubber duck or a plastic shield and then there is a bit of a barbecue and a pint and everybody goes home. And the Game Conservancy gets a few bob.

Then there are Charity shoots where there are teams of three and it costs £25 to enter and the Clay Conservation prize for the lowest scoring shooter is actually quite nice and some people actually have matching hats and there is a bit of a barbecue after with a glass of wine and then everyone goes home and the Countryside Alliance gets a few quid.

And then there is this. There is a special paddock set aside for the helicopters and there are stars of stage, screen and stadium crawling out of the woodwork. There is a commissionaire on the car park because there are so many Ferraris and Astons and Bentleys that unless some folk can remember the colour they might never find the damn thing again. The uniform is deck shoes and an ever so slightly unstructured linen suit over silk. And everybody has a drop dead Italian over and under. Forty grand a pop and just about what everyone is using now, darling. Team entry here for the four of you is a grand but you will never know because Charlie puts the team together every year and pays for everyone and you're only here because Chris had to fly to LA at the last minute and Eric was already shooting for Rory's lot and you were available and we've just got to beat the Rock Stars because if they win again they will just be insufferable.

So here's your matching shooting waistcoat and baseball cap with Charlie's Angels on the back and, yes, it is a joke but based on the fact that last year every member of Charlie's team was actually producing either a film or a musical and so they called themselves the Angels and it stuck. Except, of course, you are not producing anything just at the moment and you realise that as Mark's latest album has gone platinum and Tony's up for an Oscar, you are certainly the only member of this team who doesn't count his basic in millions and that the entry level BMW, modest side-by-side boxlock and the shooting stockings were about as serious a series of mistakes this morning as it was possible to make. Though no one says anything. Obviously.

And of course they all shoot like gods into the bargain. They haven't fired a shot since last season but as last season closed about a week ago with a series of 500 birds to your own gun dove sessions in Cordoba and a quick and dirty morning one on one yesterday just to brush up for this they still shoot straighter than you ever have or will. And stand by stand you are increasingly obviously letting the side down though everyone is frightfully nice about it and it wasn't as if a week in Nassau on a yacht was a particularly important prize even if they could have won it hands down with anyone but you and the girls would have enjoyed it after all. But not to worry.

And it only gets worse after you break for fizzy pop and canapés because the winners immediately auction their first prize and Tony promptly bids it up to nine grand because he knows that Eric will go to ten and then invite him and Charlie and the girls anyway because it's been a standing joke ever since they ended up at the North Pole together after the heads and tails two years ago. And then everybody goes home and the Prince's Trust gets a cheque for £100,000. And, boy, are you ever in the wrong place?